# The Wife's Heart

## Healing from Your Husband's Porn Addiction and Adultery

# MIKE GENUNG

Blazing Grace Publishing

PO Box 25763

Colorado Springs, CO 80936

www.roadtograce.net

*The Wife's Heart: Healing from Your Husband's Porn Addiction and Adultery*

©2017 by Mike Genung

Scripture quotations taken from the New American Standard Bible®, Copyright ©1960, 1962, 1963, 1968, 1971, 1972, 1973, 1975, 1977, 1995 by The Lockman Foundation. Used by permission. www.Lockman.org.

Scripture taken from the New King James Version®. Copyright © 1982 by Thomas Nelson. Used by permission. All rights reserved.

Cover Design ©2017 TLC Graphics, www.TLCGraphics.com.

ISBN:

978-0-9787756-7-4

0-9787756-7-8

Printed in USA.

More copies of this book can be ordered at www.roadtograce.net.

# Table of Contents

# Introduction

In 2004, when I started Blazing Grace, I assumed that most of the people we would help would be men. I was wrong. Though much of the early content I wrote was for those who struggled with sexual sin, the majority of the emails we received were from hurting wives.

Today, more than 70 percent of the inquiries we receive are from Christian women who are married to a porn-addicted husband. Most of the participants in our online forums are women. We have three times more groups for wives than we do for men. Some of their husbands have committed adultery. Many of these men are serving in the church, including pastors.

While there are many resources available for men who want freedom from sexual sin, the well dries up when it comes to their wives. Since 2000, I have seen many surveys on Christian men and porn (today, the numbers show that 65–70 percent of them are viewing it). I've *never* seen a survey that queried the wives about their husband's issues with porn, or how it's affecting them or their family. Perhaps if the women were surveyed the numbers would jump to 80 percent.

I hear "I feel utterly alone and have no one to talk to" often. Many women who've tried to reach out got hurt or spiritually abused when a Christian counselor, pastor, or trusted friend blamed her (you didn't give him enough sex) or justified her husband's actions (there's nothing wrong with porn). Then there are the wives whose husbands are raging or blaming them for their sexual sin. This happens every day in the church, where godly men are called to shun sexual sin, take responsibility for their mistakes, and care for their spouse.

If there is a forgotten subset in the church, it is the wives whose husbands are engaged in sexual sin.

In this book I'll answer the questions I hear often, including, "My husband is blaming me and won't get help—what should I do?" "Who is this man I'm married to and why is he treating me this way?" "How do I rebuild trust?" and more. We'll delve into how you can deal with triggers and overcome the spiritual battle that is set against you and your husband.

In the end, this book is about healing your heart. If I give you answers or coping methods but leave you with an empty, hurting heart, I've only given you half of what you need. Maybe less.

Ladies, this book is for you, the forgotten ones in the church. May God breathe His life and love in you through these pages.

Mike Genung

# 1

## When Your World Comes Undone

*"My husband is a pastor. Recently, I was shocked to find porn on his phone. When I confronted him, he exploded in anger and blamed me. I told him he needed to go to someone in our church. When he did, there was no accountability; our leadership never asked him to take any time off.*

*My husband went to counseling and a group, but he has not repented of his sin. He's walled off emotionally and blames me for being an unsafe person.*

*If I share my feelings He tells me what I should do to fix myself, or that I shouldn't feel that way. He blames me for his sin; he said porn is about comfort, and I don't comfort him.*

*I'm struggling with feelings of neglect from my husband, my church, and God. I've begun to see a counselor but she keeps focusing on "my codependency." It left me confused and self-doubting.*

*It's been a year of waiting, forgiving, telling my husband my needs, and confronting him. His attitude hasn't changed, and he's emotionally disengaged. Last night it hit me that we've made no progress.*

*I feel completely alone. I don't want to minister with him anymore. I'm struggling to keep my faith in God."*

We receive emails like this from hurting wives daily at Blazing Grace. Often, their stories reflect a common theme: The wife's Christian husband got hooked on porn in his teens, long before they met. They fell in love, and got married; she is unaware of his lust-habit. 10, 20, or 30 years pass, until she stumbles upon the evidence of her husband's other life, which may include porn, affairs, and/or sex with prostitutes.

The shock waves from discovering her husband is a sex addict and has been deceiving her for their entire marriage turns her world upside down. The lying and hiding upset her as much as what he did. The trauma and pain can be debilitating; one wife I know who walked in on her husband while he was having sex with a prostitute in their home ended up in a psych ward.

Her emotions are volatile; she bounces between crying, despair, and anger. Fear stalks her; will her husband act out again? Can he break free from porn? Does he even want to? Will their marriage make it? What if she ends up alone with the kids?

Her wounds are salted with insecurity.

How can she compete with those "perfect young bodies" in the videos he watched? Is he lusting after every woman he sees? Their sex life has been dead for months.

Did she lose her husband to porn because of her

perceived inadequacies?

Anger threatens to overwhelm her. Some women are walking volcanoes, while others simmer and seethe. Others try to cope by suppressing their rage, but this never works; her anger forces its way out through the cracks in her wall.

Add restoration of the marriage to her need for healing, and the road ahead seems overwhelming. What does she do if her husband blames her and refuses to get help like the pastor at the beginning of this chapter? How is trust rebuilt? What should she do if he keeps acting out? How do they rebuild their relationship... did they ever have one?

Both sides have a critical role to play. If the husband breaks free from sexual sin but his wife doesn't heal, or if she stays stuck in anger and allows bitterness to take over, the marriage can still be lost, just as it can if her husband refuses to get help and continues pursuing the ghost of lust.

The outcome can have significant eternal ramifications. After 20 years of marriage, Tina discovered her husband's sexual sin. Her rage turned white hot, then hardened into bitterness. She hated God for the husband He had given her; eventually she turned away from Him and embraced Buddhism.

Most wives won't take Tina's path, but you don't have to become a Buddhist to be crushed by the fallout of your husband's sin. Hopelessness and despair, left unchecked, can cripple your relationship with God. Though you may continue to do the things "good Christians are supposed to do" like going to church and taking care of your family, the distance between you and God will continue to grow until you reconcile with Him.

The most important part of your healing process doesn't involve your husband; your relationship with God carries the most weight. It is the Lord who will give you the strength and wisdom to navigate the emotionally charged minefield you're navigating. He is the source of healing for your heart.

Maybe you're thinking "Yeah, yeah, more religious talk, everyone says 'God loves you.' Now tell me what I need to do."

God is either real and heals the broken hearted like He says He does, or Christianity is a waste of time. He promised that when we ask for wisdom He will give it (James 1:5). He has a special place in his heart for those with a broken heart (Psalms 51:17). And He's over-the-top passionate about your marriage, even if your husband is in so deep he doesn't get it.

The Lord also said He causes all things to work together for good (Romans 8:28, even something has deeply painful as a marriage to a sex addict.

Because God is the source of your wisdom and healing, inviting Him to join you on your journey and learning how to walk with Him is woven into this book. If I just gave you the "what to dos" for dealing with your husband (which, I will) and put out a few trite clichés such as "Jesus loves you so be happy" but stopped there, your heart would still be empty, angry, or hurting, and this book would probably end up in the trash.

This journey is going to change you; a year from now you won't be the same person you were before this journey began. Some wives believe their husbands need to do all the work, while they sit back and wait until he gets it right. You can't stay where you are if you want to heal, which means change and growth.

Your faith will be stretched in ways you might not have encountered before. Faulty coping mechanisms will be exposed and need to be discarded. Your prayer life may need to be taken to the next level; distorted core beliefs must be replaced with the truth.

For the deepest healing that will produce peace and healing regardless of whether your marriage recovers or not, we'll need to examine some places in your heart that might have boarded up for a while.

When I work with men who are struggling with porn, many think they just need a few tricks for overcoming temptation and they'll be on their way. But when they see that lust has warped their entire character with sex and self-absorption, deceit and fear are imbedded into their character, their priorities are messed up, and their relationship with God and their wife has been a sham, they understand they're in for a major overhaul in every area of their life.

Surprisingly, many of them still have a baby-Christian like approach to their relationship with the Lord. When I ask them what their relationship with Him looks like, I often hear "well, I read the Bible and pray." That's like me asking them what their marriage looks like and hearing, "I take out the trash and provide for my family." They think the Christian life is about *doing their duty*, not an incredible love relationship with the most powerful Being of the universe where they experience deep joy, love, and peace.

Some Christians want to paint a rosy picture that there will always be a happy ending this side of eternity. I believe the church fails big time when it focuses exclusively on the positive side of life; we're not raising up believers with faith and character tough enough to weather every storm as it comes.

I want to equip you to be like Jael, wife of Heber, who pounded a spike in Sisera's temple (he was the commander of the Canaanite army), Abigail, wife of Nabal, who stood up to David and saved her family's lives when he was en route to kill them after Nabal's foolishness, and Esther, who put her life on the line and was used powerfully by God to deliver the nation of Israel.

These women of Biblical fame were feminine, yet strong in character and faith. They weren't looking for a fight, but didn't back away when it came their way. They had weaknesses (Esther grappled with fear and had to invite Haman and King Ahasuerus to dinner several times before she got up the courage to confront Haman) but they persevered until the battle was won.

Oh, and by the way, with the exception of John, it was the female followers of Jesus who were with Him until the end at the cross, long after the male disciples had bailed out:

*But there were standing by the cross of Jesus His mother, and His mother's sister, Mary the wife of Clopas, and Mary Magdeline.* —John 19:25

You have more hope, tools, and Holy Spirit-fueled strength and power than you realize. God has been using women of feminine strength and character who love Him to change lives since the beginning of time.

You have an open invitation to join their ranks.

# NOTES

## 2

## Who Is He?

*I just found out my husband has been messaging other women sexually and watching porn throughout our marriage. He lied the first time I confronted him.*

*Later, when I caught him, he finally confessed. I feel like my whole marriage has been a lie. He says he wants to save our marriage, but he's always angry and snaps at me.*

"How could he do this to me?"

"Why has he lied to me our entire marriage?"

"Who is my husband? Do I even know him?"

Many wives ask these questions after discovering their husband's secret world. Let's look at what sexual sin has done to him.

Men are hardwired for sex; it takes little in the way of visual stimulation to get them going. Put a sexually charged image in front of them, or a woman who's dressed provocatively in public, and their sex drive is fired up.

Sex is a powerful, bonding force. When used exclusively in marriage, the husband and his wife are united physically, emotionally, and spiritually. The gift of sex is designed by God to cement their union and keep it strong for life.

When my wife and I are clicking in our relationship and sexually active, there's nothing that can come between us.

So what does that bonding force do to a man who masturbates to porn?

Porn sparks an emotional misfire. There's no person to bond with, so he "bonds" with the person he's having sex with—himself. Simultaneously, his mind fastens to the unreal landscape of the fantasy world.

As time goes on and he continues to frolic in fantasyland, it becomes his safe haven. The unreal is now his love, his drug, his go-to when life gets tough. The "perfect" women in porn become his comfort and his excitement; they never complain and are always ready to have sex with him, how and when he wants it.

What he doesn't understand is that porn and adultery drain him. Instead of sustaining life, they take it.

*For on account of a harlot one is reduced to a loaf of bread, And an adulteress hunts for the precious life.*
—Proverbs 6:26

THIS IS WHAT PORN DOES:

1. After every use, he experiences a shame hangover that can last for days. I always felt soiled afterward, like I'd drank a quart of sewage. Over the years, shame works its way into the man's identity; he is dirty, unworthy of love. Shame alone has the power to block the receipt of true love, leaving him starved and . . .

2. Empty. For me, that miserable, hollow feeling was the worst, even more than the shame. An empty man is vulnerable to temptation; he fights his flesh with his flesh, which never works. There is no life, love, or peace. No one can withstand a vacant heart. Since his answer to pain or stress is porn, the addictive cycle of binge, shame, and misery is set in motion.

3. From the first time he used porn, lying and deceit were embedded in his character. Prior to marriage, men may boast of a woman they slept with, but you'll never hear them brag about masturbating to porn—it's always done in isolation.

Hiding and lying are two sides of the same coin. Years before he met you, your husband was training himself to live a double life. When a character flaw like deception is allowed to harden in the heart for years, it becomes second nature.

After years of successfully deceiving others, he becomes a master poser. He knows which mask to use for every situation and how to play the part. If he's with other Christians, he knows the right Bible verses to quote and how to fake humility. He may use ministry as a drug to temporarily medicate his inner misery. Comments like this are the fix he's after: "Ohhhh, brother Jim, you ministered to me this morning. God is using you powerfully. Your family must be so blessed to have a godly man like you at home!"

When I'm working with men, I'll often tell them to get out of ministry, at least temporarily. The only way to rebuild their life is if every false coping mechanism is stripped away.

4. Fear takes up residence in their heart. The idea of getting caught is terrifying. The fear of rejection and what would happen if their loved ones "really knew who they were" are powerful forces that drive them to withdraw from others. Shame, lying, and fear are connected; when one is triggered, the other two follow. Add the spiritual battle where the enemy does everything he can to keep him in bondage, and the battle can seem overwhelming.

5. Remember how we talked about the emotional misfire that occurs when a man masturbates, and how he bonds to himself? The result of self-bonding is self-absorption: "I want what I want, when I want it; if you don't give it to me now, you will pay, or I will get it on my own terms." His pride balloons. When a proud person doesn't get their way, they rage, justify, deflect, manipulate, pout, or criticize. Once he finds a method that works (such as raging or blaming), he uses it repeatedly until he wears his wife down and she becomes his slave.

6. They shut their heart down. Many men report feeling like they stopped developing emotionally when they started using porn. They avoid emotions like the

plague; negative emotions like fear or pain must be medicated with porn. A man whose emotions are closed off will struggle to empathize with his wife when she shares her feelings, expresses love, or shows affection.

7. They become angry. They hate what they've done to themselves, yet the lying and hiding are so deeply ingrained they feel trapped and unable to ask for help. He takes his misery out on his loved ones; he is critical, bitter, and aloof, prone to outbursts if the wrong subject is brought up or he is confronted.

8. They turn to other forms of medication. Some men, especially those in ministry, become raging workaholics. Gluttony, overindulgence in hobbies or sports, drugs, or alcohol are other false coping mechanisms they may resort to.

9. They lose interest in sex with their wife. Some men become so immersed in the fantasy world that it drains their desire for sex with their spouse. Since masturbating to porn is about finishing as soon as possible, they may not last long if intercourse does occur; some men may even struggle with erectile dysfunction. This adds to his shame and compounds the compulsion to withdraw and hide. It's not uncommon to hear a wife say it's been years since she last had sex with her husband.

10. Their heart hardens. Here's where it gets dangerous. Eventually, they will have to choose between God and their family, or sexual sin. Living the double life takes too much out of them; either they will set themselves against God and the conviction of the Holy Spirit, or surrender and allow Him to have His way.

Once their heart goes hard, anything can happen.

They may become verbally and physically abusive, walk out on their family, or turn away from God. They may cross boundaries that were unthinkable before, such as viewing darker forms of pornography, same-sex attraction, voyeurism, or sex with prostitutes.

Most men aren't aware of how deeply and profoundly their character has been twisted and corrupted by lust. They're blind to how they're hurting their loved ones and destroying their life and the lives of their family.

Here's how the story often plays out. Most men get hooked on porn between ages eight and their teen years. Some were introduced to it by their father. By the time he meets his wife-to-be, he's spent years in the fantasy world; lying is embedded in his character, and the other effects I've described are set in motion.

He doesn't tell his fiancée about his secret world. While their relationship is new, he may give up porn for a while. Perhaps they have premarital sex and the excitement of this new outlet for his lust temporarily sidelines his desire for porn. Like many naïve young men, he assumes that once he's married and can have God-sanctioned sex, his porn problem will fade away.

Instead, marriage intensifies the pull to lust. Once the inevitable stress between two flawed people of the opposite sex from two families with imperfect communication patterns hit, he reverts to his default pattern of porn, hiding, and lying.

As the years pass, he becomes critical, bitter, defensive, and depressed. Their sex life fades. His wife is confused and doesn't understand what is happening, or how and why the man she married has changed so much.

One day, *it* happens. She stumbles onto porn on his phone, or finds an inappropriate text message to another woman. Their relationship explodes, and now they have to pick up the pieces and figure out how to put it back together.

Perhaps you're feeling discouraged because you see who you're married to; maybe your husband has a hardened heart. Or you're in your fifties or sixties; instead of sailing into the sunset, you're starting over with the daunting task of rebuilding your marriage.

Maybe you're wondering if there's hope.

There is.

Remember who God is, and the power of the cross. He came to set captives free (Luke 4:18). He loves it when one sinner repents (Luke 15:7). He's passionate about you, your marriage, and your husband. You're not alone in this. I've watched Him set other men free, heal their wives, and restore their marriages, which means it can happen for you and your husband too, if both sides are willing to do what it takes to heal and rebuild.

Your husband is a broken, fatally flawed man. Some wives see their spouse through rose-colored glasses, or expect them to live up to an impossible standard. Your husband has the same depraved sin nature we all do, pastors included. By exposing his brokenness to you, you may be getting your first glimpse of who your husband really is, weaknesses and all. No one else will see your husband like you do. For a man who is floundering in

15

shame, this will make the instances that you respond to him in grace like a drink of cold water in the desert.

The process is going to take time. Your husband has spent years, maybe decades, immersing his mind, will, and emotions in sexual sin. It's going to take him months if not years to completely heal and learn how to walk in freedom. He needs to overhaul his life and change in multiple areas. Just learning to cope with emotions is a challenge. My books, *The Road to Grace; Finding True Freedom from the Bondage of Sexual Addiction* and *100 Days on the Road to Grace*, show what the recovery process looks like.

Finally, and for some of you, the most important point of this chapter: *No matter what your husband has said, or if he's blamed you, none of your husband's actions are your fault.* One hundred percent of the responsibility for his choices to engage in sexual sin are on him. He was ensnared in lust long before he met you, and he has willfully continued to live the double life throughout your marriage.

One wife in her seventies told me her husband, who had been a Sunday school teacher, had blamed her for his sexual sin, which included affairs and pornography, throughout the fifty years of their marriage. It broke my heart when I heard how he had abused his wife for decades by saddling her with the burden of his sin. If your husband is blaming you, he's trying to make you bear his sin so he doesn't have to face who he is. Refuse to go there. If he's played you and you've allowed him to manipulate you into taking responsibility for his sin, dump that load back in his lap.

Remember that porn corrupts a man with self-absorption, pride, anger, and emotional and spiritual blindness.

If your husband were to stand before God today, there's no way the Lord would allow him to justify his sin by blaming you. What's just as insane is that you, his wife, are the person who most wants him to abstain from porn! It's not like you put a gun to his head and told your husband to have at it.

If your husband has blamed you for his sexual sin, I want to put you at ease. He alone bears the responsibility for his illegitimate choices and actions.

*The son will not bear the punishment for the father's iniquity, nor will the father bear the punishment for the son's iniquity; the righteousness of the righteous will be upon himself, and the wickedness of the wicked will be upon himself.* —Ezekiel 18:20

# NOTES

## Who Are You?

You asked me *to write a letter about how your addiction affected me. At the time, things were a bit hazy, and I was young and didn't know what to think of everything.*

*It really flared up my insecurities. I measured myself to other women "in your eyes." I was always trying to see what you'd find more attractive in others—where my flaws were. In the beginning of our marriage, it was the worst. My insecurities plus your addiction equaled disaster.*

*I watched porn movies a few times out of curiosity to see where I was lacking in bed. In a way, it was self-torture. I wasn't good enough. I didn't measure up. What was it that you were looking at or drawn to that I couldn't fill I was constantly looking at women (probably more than you) to see if you'd notice her smaller waist, her bigger chest, her whatever.*

*I've gotten better about not letting it be "my fault." If you ever decide to go down that road again and self-destruct, it isn't going to be my fault.*

19

*It'll affect me, yes, but not like twelve years ago.*

*Your sex addiction ruined the little bit of self-esteem I had back then, and there wasn't much of it to begin with. It put me on guard for everything—I was afraid that if I wasn't "perfect" (whatever that is), you'd leave or stray.*

*I made you my everything, which was wrong, and when you cheated on me with a prostitute in 1991, it devastated me.*

*Today, I still struggle with insecurity. I'm paranoid about any pictures that might be in something we might get in the mail, or even a magazine I might want to read. It's not that I think you're going to go back to where you were, but that you'll see in that picture what you don't have in me.*

In June of 1991, two years after I married my wife Michelle, I committed adultery with a prostitute in a hotel room while away on a business trip. I had also been binging on porn daily. We started seeing a marriage counselor, and I began my search for freedom from sexual sin. Eight years later, God did an amazing work in my heart and set me free.

In 2003, wanting to understand more of how I'd affected my wife and to know where our marriage was, I asked her to write a letter to me describing her journey. Her letter begins this chapter.

In marriage, a wife gives her husband her heart, mind, and body. She is vulnerable to him like no other; he sees her strengths and her flaws. She hopes their home will be a sanctuary of intimacy and love where she can be loved and accepted.

Security is a big deal to women. Her husband makes their home a safe place when he's faithful to her, treats her with kindness and respect, and cares for and protects their family. Security is tied to trust; if she doesn't trust him, she won't feel safe.

Trust is the cornerstone of every relationship; if trust isn't rebuilt, the marriage will eventually collapse. Sex is an act of sacred union and trust, where both sides expose themselves to the other with the expectation of being loved, accepted, and cherished. Sex is enjoying your spouse and knowing him in a profound way no one else ever will. (Perhaps this is why Scripture sometimes refers to sex as the act of knowing another person; I Kings 1:4, Matthew 1:25).

Or at least, that's the way it's supposed to be.

When a man sins against his wife by committing adultery, either with porn or another person, trust and security are broken.

What was precious has been violated. Her husband has given that which belonged only to her—his heart, body, and emotions—to another woman, or an image, in the case of porn.

Fear and insecurity attack her. What does porn or this other person have that she does not? What did she do wrong? If she can't keep and attract her husband above all others, especially as something as twisted and shameful as porn, what does this mean for her identity and value as a woman?

The answers many women default to is that she must

not have been enough of a woman, emotionally or sexually, or her faults and flaws were the cause, or she failed in some other way.

As my wife did, they start comparing themselves to other women (or pictures of other women) to attempt to discover where they lack. Young women, whose bodies haven't endured multiple pregnancies, can be a source of torment.

Then there is the shame. Most people associate shame with the aftereffects men experience after a porn binge, but shame soils the wife too. Shame can come from different angles: being married to a husband who masturbates to pictures, the perception she wasn't enough for him, and how she might be seen (and judged) by other women.

Shame can come from her friends too. I've heard of women who were told stupid things from other Christians, including pastors and counselors, such as, "If you just gave him more sex, he wouldn't have this problem"; "Some of this is your fault because you're co-dependent"; or, "It's just porn; it's what they do these days."

There is also the spiritual battle. Satan will go after you when you're vulnerable, hurting, and worn out. If he can get you nodding your head in agreement with his lies of shame and blame, you will flounder in hopelessness and discouragement. His goal is to tear you, your marriage, and your faith apart any way possible.

With the emotional trauma you're enduring, the state of your marriage, and the spiritual warfare you are both faced with, recovery and healing can seem as daunting as the challenge of climbing Mount Everest.

There is a way through—you can overcome. Let's begin by driving the stakes of truth into the ground that you can hold on to during the storm.

This would be a good time to get a highlighter.


You must never define your identity, value, and self-worth by your husband's sexual sin. Think back to the last chapter. Your husband was addicted to lust long before he met you. You could have the body of a twenty-one-year-old model and he would still run to porn, because lust always leaves a man empty and starved for more.

You are not your husband's lust-fix. You're his God-ordained wife. You and your husband are one flesh. When he broke his marriage vows, it cut deep into sensitive, vulnerable places in your heart. However, you must separate who you are from what he did. If, unknown to you, your husband robbed a bank and ended up in prison for fifteen years, you would not be held responsible for his choices, especially in God's eyes, and neither would his actions define your value as a woman.

In marriage, both parties have free will. Love is wonderful, powerful, and dangerous. There is always the risk that one of you might hurt or reject the other. Life isn't the Disney movie many churches pretend it is where nothing bad happens to Christians and there's always a happy ending. You and your husband can choose to leave when times get tough, or stay and tough it out.

Your husband has been making sinful choices for

years apart from you, and you can't define who you are by his failures and blindness (or allow him to).

Maybe you're thinking, "I understand what you're saying, but it's so painful, and the insecurity and fear are driving me crazy." If you wrap all of who you are around your sin-natured husband and leave God out of the picture, fear, insecurity, and anger will steamroll you. Michelle said she made me "her everything" and confessed it was wrong in her letter.

You must define your value, identity, and self-worth by what God says about you, which is:

You are beloved of the Lord:

*So, as those who have been chosen of God, holy and beloved, put on a heart of compassion, kindness, humility, gentleness and patience.*
—Colossians 3:12

You are God's daughter.

*And because you are sons, God has sent forth the Spirit of His Son into our hearts, crying, "Abba! Father!" Therefore you are no longer a slave, but a son; and if a son, then an heir through God.*
—Galatians 4:6

(Although the verse uses the word sons, it applies to women as daughters too.)

# WHO ARE YOU?

God loves you with a love that is so overwhelming that it raises the dead:

*But God, being rich in mercy, because of His great love with which He loved us, even when we were dead in our transgressions, made us alive together with Christ (by grace you have been saved), and raised us up with Him, and seated us with Him in the heavenly places in Christ Jesus, so that in the ages to come He might show the surpassing riches of His grace in kindness toward us in Christ Jesus.*
—Ephesians 2:4

And you are your husband's wife, which is a position of honor in God's eyes:

*Marriage is to be held in honor among all, and the marriage bed is to be undefiled; for fornicators and adulterers God will judge.*
—Hebrews 13:4

*Take heed then to your spirit, and let no one deal treacherously against the wife of your youth. "For I hate divorce," says the LORD, the God of Israel, "and him who covers his garment with wrong," says the LORD of hosts. "So take heed to your spirit, that you do not deal treacherously."*
—Malachi 2:15b–16

If the Lord hates divorce, He's over-the-top with passion about your marriage. Malachi 2:15 contains a stern warning to husbands not to "deal treacherously" against their wives. Meditate on all of what that means: the God of the universe is giving men a strict warning not to hurt their wives by leaving them. He has your back.

Your role as your husband's wife is precious in God's eyes. Just because your husband is blind to how valuable you are as his wife at the present does not negate how God sees and feels about you or your role in the marriage.

Earlier this year, I spoke at a conference to a group of wives whose husbands were viewing porn or involved with other sexual sin. When I shared how God saw them as described in this chapter, one woman broke down sobbing. Others had tears running down their faces.

Many wives have been starved for love for years in their marriage; some, for all of their life (their family of origin was no better). You may not have love in your marriage, but there is a better, powerful, and everlasting love available to you, that which only comes from the Living God.

Some of you bought in to the idea that you can't be cherished or loved, or are unworthy of it, because of your husband's sexual sin. You've embraced the lie that your identity and self-worth are determined by what's going on in your marriage or family.

If we define whether we are worthy of love by the actions of others, the best we can hope for is a few moments of fleeting happiness. If you're in the middle of a marriage that's reeling from your husband's sexual sin, you may not even get that.

When God is our first love and we abide in His care

for us, though others may hurt us, we have a rock-solid anchor that will stabilize us in the midst of every trial. Fear and insecurity will have little to hold onto, and we will be more apt to hear God's voice, receive His guidance, and live in His strength.

It's important that you're able to embrace your identity through God's eyes and make Him your first source of love. If your husband is in deep with sexual sin, you'll need to be anchored to your God-given identity for the challenges we will discuss in the chapters ahead.

If you're struggling with the idea of accepting who you are in God's eyes, here's a prayer you might offer to Him. Modify or add to it as you like:

"Father, I'm struggling with accepting the truth of who You say I am. I'm realizing I've believed a lie, such as, (Fill in the blank): "I can't be loved as I am"; "You're distant or uncaring," etc.). I've defined my value as a woman by what other people have said about me or how they've treated me.

Lord, thank you that I am your beloved daughter. I'm having a hard time receiving all of what that means. Please open my heart wide to all of who I am in your eyes and what that means. Please root the truth so deeply in my heart that nothing can shake it. I love you. Please reveal yourself to me."

*And He said to her,*
*"Daughter, your faith has made you well; go in peace."*
—Luke 8:48

27

*For this reason I too, having heard of the faith in the Lord Jesus which exists among you and your love for all the saints, do not cease giving thanks for you, while making mention of you in my prayers; that the God of our Lord Jesus Christ, the Father of glory, may give to you a spirit of wisdom and of revelation in the knowledge of Him. I pray that the eyes of your heart may be enlightened, so that you will know what is the hope of His calling, what are the riches of the glory of His inheritance in the saints, and what is the surpassing greatness of His power toward us who believe.*
—Ephesians 1:15–19

# NOTES

## 4

## You and God

*God allowed me to marry a man without knowing any of
his secret life. I prayed for a godly husband, and got a
sex addict instead! So they are no longer two,
but one flesh. What therefore God has joined together, let
no man separate.*
—Matthew 19:6

In the last chapter, we looked at God's heart for you
and your marriage. You are his daughter and He loves
you deeply.

God knew your husband was a sex addict before you
married him, watched as he kept his secret world from
you, and allowed you to marry him without intervening.
As the years passed, the Lord was there as your husband
continued to deceive you and break your marriage vows.

Then, the truth was exposed, and you're left with the
broken pieces of your heart and a marriage that is on life
support.

Where are you with your relationship with the Lord?

Are you angry at Him? Do you feel tricked? Have you distanced yourself from Him from the shock, perhaps to protect yourself? Do you see Him as cruel?

Or do you see Him as your loving Father in spite of what has happened?

You need God's grace, mercy, guidance, wisdom, and comfort for the path ahead. If you have a distorted view of His character, are withdrawn from Him, or if you're so furious that you want nothing to do with Him, you will be disconnected from the One Person you need the most.

This doesn't mean you put on a happy Christian mask and pretend you're good with God. No posers allowed here. We need to examine all of what's going on in your heart for reconciliation and healing to occur.

Let's look at what's going on.

You and your husband have free will. God isn't a master puppeteer, pulling broken men and women's strings to make them do what He wants. That's a master-slave relationship, not one born of love. I don't want my wife or friends to do something for me because I coerced or manipulated them. I want it to come freely from their heart so I know their love for me is genuine.

Your husband can choose whether to indulge in porn and deceive you, or turn from his sin, get help, and love you. If your husband wants freedom from sin and is willing to do whatever it takes, he can have it because God came to set captives free (Luke 4:18).

You can choose whether you want to tough it out and work at rebuilding your marriage, or walk away and divorce your husband. You can run toward God with everything you have, or you can walk away from Him.

Free will makes life dangerous; anything can happen. You could do everything right and still lose your marriage if your husband doesn't get help. Your husband could get help and break free, yet the marriage could end in divorce if you allow bitterness to own you or don't take the steps to heal your heart.

Free will also makes life an exciting adventure. It is hard, at times miserably so, but to those who persevere and grow through the hard times, the rewards are deep and satisfying.

Some churches and Christians blow it big time because they paint a Pollyanna view of life. Many of today's Christian radio stations use marketing slogans like "positive and encouraging" in their promotional media. Churches that dwell on grace but exclude the hard side of life keep His people trapped in a bubble of unreality. Their congregations hear comfy phrases like, "God loves you and has a wonderful plan for your life," but neglect to share that Jeremiah 29:11 was spoken to the nation of Israel while they were suffering in exile in Babylon.

Then when the bottom drops out of their life, they crumble along with it because the church hasn't taught them what tough faith in the midst of suffering is about.

*If you are slack in the day of distress, Your strength is limited.*
—Proverbs 24:10

In the book of Job, God allowed Job to go through

horrific trials at the hand of Satan. He lost his business, his employees were killed, and he suffered the overwhelming sorrow of losing his children. Then God allowed Satan to torment Job physically (see the first two chapters of Job).

Job's response amazes me:

> *"Naked I came from my mother's womb,*
> *And naked I shall return there.*
> *The LORD gave and the LORD has taken away.*
> *Blessed be the name of the LORD."*
> —Job 1:20

Job must have forged a deep love relationship with God before Satan was allowed to attack him. I don't know how he could have responded otherwise.

However, Job didn't put on a Sunday happy face and pretend all was well:

> *Therefore I will not restrain my mouth;*
> *I will speak in the anguish of my spirit,*
> *I will complain in the bitterness of my soul.*
> *Am I the sea, or the sea monster,*
> *That You set a guard over me?*
> *If I say, "My bed will comfort me,*
> *My couch will ease my complaint,"*
> *Then You frighten me with dreams*
> *And terrify me by visions;*
> *So that my soul would choose suffocation,*
> *Death rather than my pains.*

*I waste away; I will not live forever.*
*Leave me alone, for my days are but a breath.*
—Job 7:11–16

*But I would speak to the Almighty,*
*And I desire to argue with God.*
—Job 13:3

*But the falling mountain crumbles away,*
*And the rock moves from its place;*
*Water wears away stones,*
*Its torrents wash away the dust of the earth;*
*So You destroy man's hope.*
—Job 14:18–19

Job told God to "leave him alone," that he wanted to "argue with God," and accused the Lord of "destroying man's hope." God didn't lightning-bolt Job for expressing his pain, confusion, and anger.

Job's response from such intense suffering was understandable. The pain also flushed out his core beliefs of how he thought life should work. If you read through the book of Job, you'll also see that Job defended his integrity multiple times. Job's theology—his beliefs about life and God—could be described as "if I do good things and please God, nothing bad will happen to me."

God blew all of that away when He gave Satan the green light to attack Job in spite of the fact that he had done nothing wrong. Then at the end of the book, instead of telling Job why he suffered, God's response could be summed up as, "I created the universe, the earth, man, every living thing, and run it all. Who are you to question Me?" Job recanted his accusations immediately after He saw God and heard Him speak.

Maybe the Lord is blowing some of your beliefs away too. He has allowed you to marry a man who, today, is addicted to sexual sin. He has allowed your husband to hurt you. Yet there is more going on than you're aware of. He's running the universe, and He knew what He was doing when He put the two of you together. His character is still rock solid, and you can trust Him. If you want to.

Pride is often our biggest hindrance to seeing God as He is. "Look at how I've lived my life for you! You owe me God! You should have given me a spouse who wouldn't hurt me, kids who appreciate me, friends who don't say stupid things, a church that gets it right all of the time, and no suffering or pain!"

Since the day Adam and Eve chose to sin (free will), every human being has been fatally flawed with an evil sin nature. God let us have what we wanted, and it blew up in our face. Your husband has this same curse.

So do you.

It's the grace, forgiveness, and love of God that gives hope, heals hearts, and restores marriages. He didn't leave us alone; instead, when we go through suffering, He extends His hand and says, "I love you. If you allow Me to walk with you on your journey, I will help you."

Walking with you means He will take you through, not out of, the pain. He will guide you, provide wisdom, encourage you, and give you rest. He will also strengthen you so that you can endure, grow, and overcome.

*Do not fear, for I am with you; Do not anxiously look*
*about you, for I am your God. I will strengthen you,*
*surely I will help you, Surely I will uphold you with My*
*righteous right hand.*
—Isaiah 41:10

*But if any of you lacks wisdom, let him ask of God, who*
*gives to all generously and without reproach, and it will*
*be given to him.*
—James 1:5

*The LORD is my shepherd,*
*I shall not want.*
*He makes me lie down in green pastures;*
*He leads me beside quiet waters.*
*He restores my soul;*
*He guides me in the paths of righteousness*
*For His name's sake.*
—Psalm 23:1–3

So what does walking with God look like?

It begins with surrender: "Okay, Lord, no matter what happens, even if I lose my marriage, I will trust you. I give you my heart, my husband, and my marriage to do with as you like. My hand is off the controls. Please give me what I need every day and walk with me. Reveal your love and grace to me. Teach me and please help me to obey."

Such a prayer puts pride . . . self . . . to death, and gives the Lord freedom to work your heart. It's also the catalyst to grace:

*But He gives a greater grace. Therefore it says, "GOD IS*
*OPPOSED TO THE PROUD, BUT GIVES GRACE TO THE*
*HUMBLE." Submit therefore to God. Resist the devil and*
*he will flee from you. Draw near to God and He will*
*draw near to you.*
—James 4:6–8

Wrapping our hands tightly around the steering wheel throws the vessel off course; our tendency to insist on doing life our way is fraught with problems because of our distorted motives and flesh-propelled blind spots. Often, we make the mess bigger than before.

Walking with God involves consistent prayer, listening to Him in silence, immersing your mind and heart in His word daily, personal worship, and obedience.

If your heart is to know God and His will and you go after Him, He will speak to you. He does this through prayer, His word, circumstances, people, and in silence and solitude.

"One and done" doesn't work here. Some Christians have the attitude that "Well, I prayed once or twice, and God didn't show up. Back to doing it my way." That's not surrender, but pride on rampage: "You owe me, God, and didn't do what I wanted when I wanted it."

Those who are hungry for God go after Him until He shows up, no matter how long it takes. They understand He hears and receives every prayer, and are okay waiting for His answer. Knowing and loving God is worth the wait, just as waiting for their spouse was before they got married.

I believe God hears every prayer and works through it. Sometimes, my circumstances don't change, but I do. Maybe I toughen up a little so that what was weak is now strong, my heart softens, or I come to a place of rest and trust in spite of the insanity that's swirling around me.

When we pray, a part of our goal is to get our heart in line with His:

*and whatever we ask we receive from Him, because we keep His commandments and do the things that are pleasing in His sight.*
—I John 3:22

This verse brings us back to obedience. As you walk with God, He will show you the next step (not the full plan); then you will have to choose whether to obey or not. Disobedience can mean staying stuck, or worse, it may bring about hard consequences.

I have never regretted obeying God. There have been situations when I knew God was calling me to do something that freaked me out and took me way out of my comfort zone, but every time I took the plunge and obeyed, it always turned out to be the right way to go.

Obedience is far better than all the guilt and crummy feelings that come with knowing we're pulling a Jonah and going the opposite way from what God told us to.

Knowing God's will can take time. Don't take the first thought or verse that pops into your mind as if it's from Him. Learn to discern between God's voice, your flesh, and the enemy with persistent prayer and time in His word. If you think you're hearing from God but don't have clarity or a firm sense on the direction you should take, wait. Keeping praying and seeking, and ask for the input of other trusted, mature believers.

I suggest that you park here for a bit. Get alone with the Lord, and pour out your heart to Him, just as Job did. Journaling is helpful. Examine your beliefs about God's character and how you see Him. Ask Him to expose any resentment, anger, or discouragement that you need to work out with Him. Then look for the truth of His character as revealed in His word, and spend time resting in His presence.

# NOTES

 5

## Who Should I Tell?

It's hard to *find support. Anywhere. Some just laugh and say, "Porn is normal." Others judge us. We went to our pastor, but this was a waste of time; my husband felt like the pastor blew him off.*

*He who separates himself seeks his own desire,*
*He quarrels against all sound wisdom.*
—Proverbs 18:1

*Therefore, confess your sins to one another, and pray for one another so that you may be healed. The effective prayer of a righteous man can accomplish much.*
—James 5:16

One of the worst things you can do is walk this road alone. Allowing your emotions to fester and build is like covering a volcano with a lid and hoping it doesn't blow the top off.

You need a safe person outside of your marriage who will walk with you without judging, trying to fix you or your husband, or pouring gasoline on the fire. Friends aren't always a good choice. One wife whose husband was a sex addict told me she had to distance herself from her friends because they kept telling her to divorce him. Her husband later broke free, and their marriage was restored.

The wife's comments at the top of this chapter are not rare; in fact, they may be the norm, in and outside of the church. Many non-believers don't see a problem with pornography. I heard one secular psychologist say that porn wasn't a problem; it was "the addiction" that was bad. That's like saying cocaine or heroin are okay; it's just when you get hooked (which usually happens), it becomes a problem.

Then there is the church. I've heard all sorts of goofy, crazy words that have spewed out of would-be Christian counselors over the years. Some prescribe, "Take two verses, pray, and call me in the morning." Most men have prayed and Bible-read their brains out and gotten nowhere, including seminary-educated, Greek-reading, porn-addicted pastors.

Some counselors tell a wife her husband wouldn't have this problem if she gave him enough sex, was nicer, wasn't codependent, or (fill in the blank). I have yet to hear of one story of a wife who made a change that fixed her husband's lust problem.

Some Christians freak out when it comes to sex. In 2000, four years before starting Blazing Grace and writing my first book, I started a Christ-centered support group for men who wanted freedom from sex addiction. I found a book I wanted to use for study in the group, went to a large Christian bookstore, and grabbed six copies. When I placed them in front of the cashier, who was a lady in her fifties, she quickly stuffed the books in a paper bag as if I were buying porn. The cover of the book had a large picture of a dove on the front and was as innocent looking as they come.

What's wrong with Christians when it comes to discussing sex? The world shoves its depraved version of sexuality down our throats.

You can't go to most grocery stores without getting exposed to a wall of soft-core porn on the magazine covers at the cash register. We shouldn't have a problem standing up and proclaiming God's standards on sex— after all, He addresses it in His word many times, often in clear terms:

*Let your fountain be blessed, and rejoice in the wife of your youth. As a loving hind and a graceful doe, let her breasts satisfy you at all times; Be exhilarated always with her love.*
—Proverbs 5:18–19

The unfortunate truth is that the church isn't often a safe place to receive help for sexual issues. Many have no training or experience in this arena. They don't know the right questions to ask, what the key issues are, or what to do with them.

I do not recommend telling your family, especially in the beginning when your marriage is in a raw, fragile state. Your relatives are emotionally invested and may have a hard time being impartial, supporting you and your husband, and withholding their opinions on what they think you need to do to fix your relationship. Telling dear Aunt Betty who can't keep her nose out of everyone's business and has it in for your husband is the wrong move.

Telling your parents about your husband's sexual sin will heap more shame on your husband (as well as you) at a time when both of you are trying to recover from it. If you think it's needed, you can tell your family later, perhaps in a year or two after you've both healed.

You and your husband need safe people who will help cultivate your healing process, not hinder it. Safe people:

* Listen first. They focus on trying to understand you, not fix you. Good listeners ask lots of questions. They don't offer advice until they've earned the right by investing the time to make sure you know you've been heard, or you've asked for their input.

* Don't preach. They lay off the mini-sermons.

* Can keep what's said confidential. They won't go to their friends, relatives, or pastor and say, "Psst . . . we need to pray for Jim and Susy because Jim's into porn and Susy's cracking up."

* Stay away from cheap clichés like, "God never gives you more than you can handle" (He gives us more than we can handle so we see our desperate need to rely on and walk with Him) or "God's in control." Yes, God's in control, but telling that to a suffering person who may be struggling with their faith is like saying, "Cheer up! God is allowing you to get the living daylights kicked out of you!"

* Don't freak out with topics like sex. They're grounded in the real world and don't have a problem discussing the tough issues.

* Have suffered. The best counselors are those who have walked through their own trials and pain and have come through it. They usually have more wisdom and understanding than a professional with a trail of letters behind their name.

It's not uncommon to hear of someone who's spent years and thousands of dollars on a licensed counselor and has made no progress. I've heard of counselors whose approach is to say, "What would you like to discuss today?" at the beginning of each session. A person who's lost in the confusing world of healing their marriage from sexual sin needs guidance, not an open-ended chat—or a counselor whose motive is to keep their client coming back.

Here are suggestions on finding safe persons or counselors:

Start with prayer. Ask God for the right person(s), group, or counselor to work with. He has your best interest in mind and knows the right person.

If you're thinking of talking to a friend, probe them on their beliefs about porn, sexual sin, adultery, and what helping people looks like. Have they walked through their own path of suffering? How is their bitterness meter? Are they quick to judge others when they fall? Can they keep what is shared confidential? Can they talk about sex without crawling under the table?

If, after praying and asking these questions, you think you might want to proceed with them, don't dump all of your story in one sitting. Give them a few pieces and see how they respond. If they start ranting about your husband or going sideways on you, it's best to stop there.

You only need one good friend you can talk to on a weekly basis. Face-to-face meetings for coffee or a meal are best; if this isn't possible, a phone call is good. Emails or texts should only be used for scheduling meeting times. Ask your friend to pray for you consistently; prayer is a key part of your healing process (James 5:16).

I meet with a Christian brother every Friday for mutual accountability and encouragement. Masks aren't allowed. My friend and I shoot straight with each other on our weaknesses, failures, and needs for prayer, as well as our victories. This is what you're after. It's how the body of Christ is meant to function. We're half-dead when we try to live the Christian life on our own.

If you're thinking of approaching your pastor or a counselor at your church, tread carefully. You can start by telling them you have a sensitive issue you need help with, but you need to ask questions first to see if they would be a good fit.

Ask them general questions on their approach in helping people, perhaps with a parallel issue like physical or sexual abuse that won't tip them off to what you're going through. Ask if they have successful experience helping couples, what their process looks like, and for examples of the end results. If you can get a reference, even better.

If they get impatient with your questions or frustrated that you won't disclose everything up front, bail out. They've already shown you they're not someone you want to work with.

If you like their responses, you might give them a piece or two of what you're going through, and see how they respond. Use the Hansel and Gretel approach of giving them a few crumbs at a time to get a feeling of whether they're capable or safe. Afterward, if you want to proceed, ask them how they would lead you and your husband to healing.

The best professional counselors are those who've struggled with sexual sin and overcome it, or who are or were a spouse of a sex addict. If they were married to a sex addict but lost their marriage to divorce, don't write them off. Remember, both sides have to choose recovery and freedom, and it may be that their spouse chose sexual sin and refused to get help. Counselors who haven't worked their way through their own road of suffering and trial will often default to working their education on you. It will be like talking to a book.

If you're thinking about working with a professional counselor, ask them about their background, how they would walk you and your husband to healing, their beliefs about pornography and adultery, if they've been able to lead other wives or couples to healing, and their stance on Scripture and how it is integrated into their counseling. Ask as many questions as possible up front, and get references if possible.

Finally, there are support groups. You want to look for a support group that is specifically for wives of sex addicts, not a one-size-fits-all support group for a woman with any issue. Then look at their structure. Is it biblical?

What do they focus on? Do they allow the wives to go at it in a free-for-all emotion dump, or do they help their group members move toward healing?

Some wives' groups are little more than volcano sessions where the wives blow up and go home. Ask what materials they use and read them. Do they incorporate prayer into their meeting times? Does the group leader help the wives see their blind spots, equip them to cope with their husbands, and point them toward Christ for healing?

It is possible to find a safe person, group, or counselor to work with. Asking as many of the right questions as possible up front well help you avoid wasting your time with the wrong one.

The person or group you work with will play a critical role in your journey. Their feedback, input, and the materials they suggest can help or damage the recovery and healing process for you and your husband. Proceed cautiously and prayerfully.

If the other person or group isn't a good fit, don't waste time trying to make it work or feel guilty for leaving. Keep moving.

Don't allow the fear of sharing with the wrong person paralyze you into keeping yourself walled off in isolation. You need the help of at least one other person outside of your marriage.

Making your husband your only source of help loads all of the stress and pressure in your marriage, making it susceptible to frequent explosions. You both need outlets outside of your marriage to process your emotions and receive support.

## WHO SHOULD I TELL?

At Blazing Grace we offer online forums, international wives' phone support groups, and counseling, as well as an international men's course. For more information, see the end of this book, or go to www.blazinggrace.org.

# NOTES

## 6

## Two + Three

*I'm scared to let my husband into my heart again; trust is miles away. He acts like everything is fine, and resents me when I tell him I'm still hurting over his repeated porn use. He lied about it again recently, right after I caught him. I don't want to be angry or bitter, but I also won't be his prostitute.*

In this chapter, we will put the man you married as described in chapter two together with the woman you are as described in chapter three, look at some scenarios, and how you might deal with them.

First, consider how sexual sin has affected your husband's character. How far along is he in the progression? Does he show signs of humility and brokenness, coupled with the willingness to answer any of your questions without dodging, getting defensive, or blowing up?

Has he been in too deep for too long to the point where his heart is hard and he refuses to get help or listen to you? Does he rage when you ask him the hard questions? Is he close to being abusive? (Is he already there?)

Or is he somewhere in the middle, with a little bit of all the characteristics mentioned above?

Now remember who you are: beloved daughter of God, the most important person in your husband's life, and his wife, which is a highly esteemed position in God's eyes.

As we get into the next two chapters, it will be important for you to maintain clarity and focus on who you are and what your marriage is, especially if your husband's heart is hard or if he's manipulating or raging. Being anchored to the truth of who you are and how valuable your role is will give you the strength to calmly yet firmly stand your ground if needed.

Hopefully, your husband's heart is pliable, even broken over his sin, and he's willing to do whatever it takes, now, to break free from lust and heal your marriage. If that's your situation, give thanks to God because there are many men who have gone too far for too long and have hardened their hearts.

For a man to break free from lust requires that:

1. They meet with another man or group at least once a week for accountability. For the first ninety days, I recommend they call their accountability partner once a day.

2. They make and execute an action plan to remove all of the stumbling blocks of temptation that are under their control. For example, if they've been viewing porn on their smartphone, they need to downgrade to a

dumbphone or install an app that 100 percent guarantees they cannot access porn. If they've been watching cable movies at home, the cable TV service gets turned off.

3. They set up weekly or biweekly appointments with you where you can ask them any question related to how they're doing with lust. This is a critical part of rebuilding trust.

4. All lying and hiding must stop.

5. They work to resolve the heart issues that drive lust. This manifests in distorted core beliefs such as, "I cannot be loved as I am"; "Lust will provide my emotional needs"; and others.

There is more to the recovery process, but these are the nonnegotiable steps your husband must take on an ongoing basis that you should be aware of. Your marriage doesn't have a chance of healing and rebuilding trust without them. Your starting point is to discover how serious your husband is about getting help as evidenced by whether he is taking these steps consistently.

During this process, your husband will have faced his brokenness, realized how he has hurt you, taken ownership for it, and started working to treat you better. You should see changes in his character, albeit slowly.

Let's take several possible scenarios you might encounter and how you could respond. These wouldn't apply to the broken and repentant husband who is in the recovery process, but those who are blaming and/or justifying their sin and refusing to get help.

Let's say you recently discovered your husband viewed porn again and has been lying about it. He hasn't taken the five steps above, or, he's not been consistent or dabbled in them.

After the discovery, you sit down with your husband to discuss what needs to happen to restore your relationship and heal your heart, especially in the area of trust. You begin to mention the five steps above, and he:

1. Blows up. This is a smoke screen meant to distract and discourage you from requiring him to get help. Think back to before you were married. If your husband had said, "Hey, I'm going to look at porn during our marriage, have an affair, and chat online with other women. You good with that?" how would you have responded? You would have flipped out and been gone. There's no way you would have considered marrying someone who wasn't 100 percent committed to being faithful to you.

Now that your husband has made vows before you and God and entered into a marriage covenant, why would you consider accepting anything less than complete faithfulness, now that you have the God-honored position as his wife?

*You have heard that it was said, "YOU SHALL NOT COMMIT ADULTERY" but I say to you that everyone who looks at a woman with lust for her has already committed adultery with her in his heart.*
—Matthew 5:27–28

Porn is emotional and physical adultery; fantasizing about having sex with another woman while having sex with self. As his wife, you are 100 percent within your rights to demand that he get help by taking the five steps immediately. Anything less is for you to enable and even condone your husband treating you like a mistress, or worse, a prostitute.

You have to force the issue to a black-and-white choice with your husband: he must choose which one he wants: sexual sin or you. He can't have both. You, as a beloved daughter of Christ and his bride, will not allow anything less.

What happens in many marriages where a husband has brow-beaten or manipulated his wife into acceptance of his sexual sin is that the wife loses confidence in herself, doesn't understand her identity, and ceases to treasure the value of their marriage. The enemy does his part and beats her up too.

Then when her hard-hearted husband blames, blows up, denies, or justifies, she backs down. Eventually, she stops fighting and freefalls into despair or depression.

If your husband reacts this way, your response should be something like this: "No, I'm not buying it. I'm your wife and when we got married, you made a vow to be faithful to me. Porn (or whatever sexual sin he's involved in) is adultery and is clearly sin in the Bible (you can reference Matthew 5:27–28 if you want). It hurts me and I won't tolerate it in our marriage. You have to choose which one you want: me or porn. You can't have both. If you want me, you're going to have to get help, and I expect you to take these five steps immediately."

If he starts freaking out and screaming, simply reiterate your position, and if he still keeps going, leave the room or the house. When they're in that place and keep baiting you, their goal is to draw you into a big fight so they can blow up the smoke screen. Don't fall for it or get manipulated into taking a rabbit trail that will cause you to deviate from the root issue that he can't have you and sexual sin.

2. Blames you by saying you aren't giving him enough sex, being nice to him, supportive, etc. I've never heard of a wife who got turned on for sex while knowing her husband was having an affair or masturbating to porn. If he's doing this, he's the sex-killer, not you. Go back to the end of chapter two: his choices are 100 percent his responsibility; he has no ground to stand on before you or God. Don't back down and allow him to guilt you into submission.

3. Refuses to get help. Some men may say something like, "Awww, I don't need help. I can do this on my own." Yeah, right. If that were true he would have stopped a long time ago. I've never heard of a guy who was in bondage to sexual sin who was able to break free without taking the five steps. Many have tried, including me. What it often boils down to is pride: they don't want to take off the mask in front of others and confess that they're not the Holy Joe Christian they've pretended to be. If he refuses to get help, what he's really doing is choosing sexual sin over you, which you must not accept.


Here's another scenario. Perhaps your husband starts getting help and making progress, but you're still hurting and angry. He comes to you and says, "Why can't you get over this?"

Remember how his character has been deformed as shown in chapter two? His self-absorption has surfaced. He's showing you he's still in Me Mode and doesn't want to deal with your pain—which he caused by years of sinning against you.

Some wives beat themselves up because they "can't get over it." They think they should be able to bounce back quickly, perhaps in a few months, and then everything will be back to normal.

It doesn't work that way. You've experienced one of the most traumatic events of your life: the betrayal and infidelity of your husband. Complete healing can take years. The process is extended if your husband slips repeatedly or doesn't treat you with kindness and care.

Don't allow either of you, your husband or yourself, to beat you up for the time it takes for you to heal. Everyone's personality, backstory, and circumstances are different; don't compare your journey to that of others. Allow yourself the freedom to heal at the timing and pace you need.

If you're in a place where you need to confront your husband on his need to get help to restore your marriage, I encourage you to read the next chapter before doing so, as it ties into this one.

# NOTES

# 7

## Boundaries, Consequences, and Control

*Our marriage has been nothing but lies. I know God commands us to forgive others. I can forgive my husband, but my feelings toward him are not the same as before. Some days, I see him as a broken man, a sinner just like me in need of grace. Others, as a man in habitual sin, which worries me about his salvation. Occasionally, I see him as an instrument Satan is using to destroy our family.*

*Then there are the days I look at my husband, and cry.*

Perhaps you read the last chapter and thought, "Wow, that's pretty harsh. I'm not sure I could be so tough with my husband or hold the line like that." Maybe his previous responses have been withering, or he's always come up with the right words to undercut what you know is right.

Every man needs grace, forgiveness, and mercy to heal from sexual addiction. If your husband has a hard heart and is justifying his sin, he needs the grace of tough love. Anything less is like watering a brick—his heart isn't in a state where he can absorb love.

Many men have told me they needed their wives to confront them and stand firm on the demand that their husband get help. The emotional and spiritual fog they're in is so thick and dark that they don't see what they're doing to themselves or their wives. Your refusal to back down may be the catalyst that sparks healing and restoration in your marriage.

There are two parts to setting boundaries. The first is to establish the boundary and provide your expectations for any action steps that might be needed to resolve the issue. The second is to back your boundaries up with consequences.

Let's look at some of those boundaries, the action steps your husband may need to take to resolve the issue, and my suggestions for appropriate consequences. Pray for wisdom about the consequences God wants you to have in place if your husband crosses your boundaries. Every marriage is different; so are the circumstances. I believe the consequences for some boundary violations (such as an adulterous relationship) should be nonnegotiable, while for others there is room for flexibility.

It's best that you predetermine your boundaries and consequences before discussing them with your husband. If he's unwilling to take the action steps necessary, the consequences must be immediate. Delays in putting them in place will show your husband you're not serious, or give him time to cajole you into backing down. It's important that you realize your marriage may depend on setting and enforcing your boundaries.

**Issue:** Your husband has been having affairs and/or sex with prostitutes. This may include an emotional affair where there was no or little physical contact, but your husband has given a piece of his heart to another woman.

**Boundary:** Sex or inappropriate relationships with other women are not acceptable and must cease immediately.

**Action steps:** He must cut off all contact with such women and do whatever it takes to avoid them. If he was having an affair with a coworker, your husband must be willing to consider quitting his job and finding another. Your marriage and your husband's holiness and obedience are a far bigger priority to God than his income. If a job change needs to be considered, the two of you should work out a plan together.

**Consequence:** If your husband is unwilling to take the action steps needed to cut off all contact, move out of the house immediately or ask him to move out. He's showing you he wants you and other women; he cannot have both.

**Issue:** Your husband rages, manipulates, or blames you for his sexual sin.

**Boundary:** Blaming you for his sexual sin is not acceptable. He must take 100 percent ownership for it. Anything less allows him to continue to abuse and bully you; it's also a sign he isn't serious about doing away with lust. Your expectation is that he will begin to work at treating you with respect.

**Consequence:** In-home separation, meaning you sleep in separate rooms. If the husband continues to blame, deflect, or justify, it is possible he is also continuing to act out sexually. Usually the men who blame aren't getting help, which is another sign he's still playing with lust. If this continues, you may need to consider separation outside of the home.

**Issue:** Lying.

**Boundary:** Your husband must be accountable to you for how he is doing with sexual sin, and answer all of your questions truthfully. He needs to understand that trust is the cornerstone of your marriage and without trust, you have no relationship. All lying must cease.

Your husband has spent years ingraining dishonesty into his character and has formed the habit. Shame and fear are powerful enemies whose mission is to keep him in hiding. Many men keep the truth from their wives because they're terrified of what her response will be.

For many women, lying is as bad as what their husbands did. Before you discuss consequences, help him understand how important honesty is to you. You might also share how it affects or hurts you when he lies.

**Consequence:** In the beginning, after discovering a lie, you may consider showing grace to encourage him to choose honesty and reinforcing how important it is to you. Remember the shame he's been ensnared to. If he keeps lying, you'll need to move toward drawing a hard line in the sand.

If you've discussed your expectation for the truth from him in the past and he's lied repeatedly, you may consider a "no-lying policy" from today forward.

The consequences can start small with a warning ("If you keep lying, I can't trust you . . . we'll need to sleep in separate rooms the next time it happens.") to sleeping in separate rooms, and then, taking more drastic action, such as moving out.

Lying can be a sign of your husband hiding sexual sin, or it can solely be a character defect he needs to work through, meaning he's abstinent from sexual sin but needs work in this area. Some men have an easier time being honest after they've been able to find freedom from shame and fear. Take your husband's past, the action steps he's taking, and his current state of humility into consideration when prayerfully setting a consequence for this one.

**Issue:** Porn and masturbation.

**Boundary:** Both stop. Masturbation short-circuits the sex life between a husband and wife, while porn is adultery. Your expectation for porn use should be that your husband takes the five steps mentioned in the last chapter immediately and consistently for at least two years.

There's a lot going on here for you to consider before determining your consequences. If he's spent years or decades acting out with porn, he has a long, hard road ahead of him to freedom. Significant life change will be required. This isn't going to be an overnight process, and he will need your grace and support.

Having said this, his porn habit is painful for you. If he's not willing to take the five steps immediately and consistently, he's playing games, which you must not tolerate. I would suggest either in-home separation or one of you leaving.

If he gets plugged into groups and starts taking the other steps but stumbles, I would extend grace as long as he's making progress. If he's viewing porn on a consistent basis, which I define as once every week or two, it probably means he isn't doing enough to cut off the temptation points of lust under his control (such as downgrading to a dumbphone) and should trigger a discussion with him on what he needs to do to eliminate the temptation, or, if he's unwilling to take action, a consequence on your part.

If he stumbles, step back and pray for the discernment to understand if he's sincere, working hard, and making progress (albeit with some mistakes along the way), or if he's not committed and just playing games. Ask questions and try to learn as much as you can before making a decision. Sometimes they need a little help navigating the fog, and you can help him see his blind spots.

For several years, I met with Bill once a week for the purpose of accountability. Bill was in his late fifties, married, and masturbating to porn once every one to two weeks. After two years of challenging Bill to do something serious about his smartphone, which he was viewing porn on, and watching him slip, I told him I could no longer meet with him as an accountability partner because he didn't want to take the action steps necessary to cut lust off.

To my knowledge, Bill, now in his sixties, is still addicted to porn.

Bill, by the way, wasn't telling his wife about his porn habit. He told her occasionally (once every four to five months) in a non-specific way ("I'm struggling") about his porn use, but that was as close as it got.

Guys like Bill need consequences to wake them up. They also need wives who will ask them the hard questions once every one to two weeks to keep them focused.

In Bill's case, his wife should have started with in-house separation, and then progressed to moving out if he didn't take action.

**Issue:** Physical abuse—defined as striking you with force.

**Boundary:** Zero tolerance.

**Consequence:** This is what happens when a man allows his heart to harden to the point where his anger has taken over and transformed to rage. You should have a zero-tolerance policy when it comes to physical abuse. If it happens once, leave, at least for several days. Don't return until he commits to getting into counseling and attending a support group.

If he grabs you by the arm, you might consider warning him that you're gone if he does it again.

Strangling or hitting are nonnegotiable: if he does it once, leave.

In the past two chapters, we've looked at what confronting your husband and setting boundaries looks like. Now let's look at the best way to approach him.

If you need to confront him, work to keep your emotions in control and speak in a tone that is kind yet firm.

*A gentle answer turns away wrath, but a harsh word stirs up anger.* —Proverbs 15:1

If you go at your husband with both guns blazing, screaming, and spraying him with four-letter words and insults, he's going to fight back (especially if he's prone to outbursts) or withdraw into a shell and "yes dear" you. Either way, you don't have a shot at getting the message through.

When a wife goes to her husband in kindness, she shows him she's on his side. Her starting position of grace opens the door for him to confess his sin and work with her. Most husbands will be far more convicted (even if the conviction comes later) if their wives approach them in love. When Michelle has confronted me in kindness after I did something wrong, it melted my heart. Her purity and holiness as a daughter of Christ soaked me in conviction.

This doesn't mean your husband will respond in kind. Some won't. Focus on staying above reproach in

God's eyes. Do your part to communicate the truth in love, and then let the Lord have the results.

Pray before you talk with your husband, and ask God to shower both of you with grace. Bring God into the entire process. It's important that you don't do this in the weakness of your own strength. I also encourage you to ask your (safe) friends to pray for you and your husband.

There is a difference between setting a boundary and trying to control your husband to force him to do what you want. A boundary gives him the free will to choose to get help or change. You're not his puppet master; the goal is for him to want to choose to take the action steps on his own. It won't last long if you've manipulated him.

A boundary morphs into control when the wife tells her husband what he will do, when, and how.

Here's what control looks like: the wife sets the boundary that her husband must take the five steps, and then says, "You will go to the men's weekly Bible study at our church, the sex addiction group I found online, and see Billy Joe Bob, who is my mother's counselor, once a week."

Trying to control your husband will blow up in your face. If he doesn't rebel (which, he should, because he would be setting a healthy boundary with you), he may fake it and play along for a while, but eventually, he'll quit.

You want your husband to step into the battle and stay there until he's victorious because he wants to, not from resentment because his wife went control freak on him. Your husband should be given the freedom to make the decisions on which groups and counselors he works with.

If you're trying to control your husband and he's balking and refusing to play along, that's a healthy step on his part. Step back and allow him the grace to go after God's will for his path of healing.

If he's open to it, you can ask him if he'd like you to look for groups for him, or you might share some resources you've found. Offering him information is helping him; crossing into "you will see this counselor" violates the boundary.

Many wives try to control their husbands because of fear or pride. Fear is a merciless slave master; it will keep you cowering in the corner so that you're ineffective in your God-given role as your husband's wife, or compel you to provoke or clutch at him until he backs away. We'll talk more about putting fear into submission in a future chapter.

Pride says, "I know what you need and you need to do this my way. If you don't, you're going to get it and I will never forgive you." Pride isn't surrendered to God; it always insists on being in control.

Pride is about revenge, not mercy; pain, not healing; it is a rampaging bull that stampedes everything in its path.

When someone doesn't do what Pride wants, it goes postal. If your husband has blown up at you in the past, you know it's no fun to be on the receiving end when Pride is driving your spouse.

Living in humility and surrender is the best way for

you to keep Pride at a distance. God is your husband's judge, not you. Do what you know God is calling you to do, and then step back and allow Him the room to work in your husband's heart.

# NOTES

## Triggers, Triggers, Everywhere

*My husband says he is fine now that God has forgiven him, and doesn't need an accountability partner. He said I should be "over his little porn habit." I still have outbursts of anger; my emotions are easily triggered. I have forgiven him and pray all the time for God to help us both. I wonder if he is being honest with me since he says he's fine every day and nothing affects him anymore. As far as seeing beautiful young girls or anything that could trigger him. Does anyone understand how I feel? I have such a hard time with insecurity and fear.*

In 1991, several weeks after I'd committed adultery with a prostitute, Michelle and I went to see a movie. Without knowing the content, we chose Dutch, about a man played by Ed O'Neil who is dating a divorced woman. In one scene, while Dutch is parked in his car, a prostitute opens the back door and jumps into the backseat.

That scene hit Michelle hard, and she started crying. I felt horrible and wanted to crawl into a hole. The rest of the day was spent in confused, tormented silence, with me not knowing what to say and my wife treading water.

One year later, Michelle and I were visiting a couple. As the husband, a Christian, was watching a movie, a sexually charged scene came on with female nudity. The moment that scene hit, I turned away until it was over (my friend's eyes were glued to the screen). When I looked up at Michelle, she mouthed the words "thank you." What could have triggered her pain and insecurity turned out to be a good thing when she saw that I honored her by handling temptation the right way.

Let's look at some triggers and what causes them:

1. A young woman passes you on the street. She's dressed with a shirt that's cut too low and tight pants that offer way too much flesh.

You've had multiple pregnancies, and have the scars to show for it. Insecurity spears your heart, and you compare yourself to her. Your mind wanders to your husband's obsession with porn, and you continue the impossible-to-win comparison game until you've dug yourself into a hole of discouragement and despair.

2. Repeat that scenario, but this time you're with your husband. As you approach a young woman, out of the corner of your eye, you see that your husband is a little nervous. His eyes dart back and forth. Is he lusting after her? Comparing this girl to you and what you "lack"? Waves of anger roll over you. You're seething at

the girl for how she's dressed and your husband for his weakness.

3. Your husband is late from work and hasn't called. In the past, you've discovered inappropriate texts to other women on his smartphone. He's told you he's cut off all contact with them, but how do you know if you can trust him? Fear spiders down your spine. Is he texting another woman? Or worse, meeting one? As the downward spiral accelerates into obsessive worry, fear sinks its fangs deeper into your heart. By the time your husband comes home, you're in the throes of an anxiety attack.

When it comes to triggers, the Big Four are fear, anger, insecurity, and pain. Fear run amok can lead to anxiety and panic attacks. Some women end up on antidepressants or other medications because their nervous systems are fried.

Unchallenged insecurity can drive you into depression and discouragement, and maybe more meds.

If you invite anger to take residence in your heart instead of allowing it to pass through, it will fester into bitterness and harden your heart.

Then there is your wound. How do you protect it from being salted by outside forces?

Let's unpack all of this and cut these triggers down to size.

You've been hurt by your husband's sexual sin; the pain can hit without warning, bringing you to tears. This is the natural result of what happens when a heart has been wounded. Your pain is nothing to be ashamed of, and you should allow yourself the time it takes to heal, just as you would if you'd fractured a bone.

Being angry at your husband is okay, even a good thing. Anger, when expressed in a non-abusive way, can provide release for your emotions and positive change in your spouse. He needs to understand how profoundly you've been hurt. Ephesians 4:26 tells us to "be angry and do not sin." We're not called to be dispassionate mice, but lovers of God and our spouse. Anger can be a positive sign of your passion and love for your husband.

Fear is a direct assault on your heart meant to keep you isolated, withdrawn, ineffective, and spiritually blind. Fear is the opposite of faith, and is a trust-killer. It chokes our relationship with God and blocks the ability to rebuild trust with our spouse. Fear probes until it finds a weakness; once a soft spot is discovered it violently drills a hole and sets an anchor. Fear is never your friend unless it is in the one God-given context given in Scripture: the fear of the Lord, which is the beginning of wisdom (Proverbs 9:10).

Fear is one of Satan's most powerful weapons. He uses it to immobilize you, cripple your faith, hammer the wedge of distrust deeper in your relationship with your husband (and God, if he can), and set you on fire with anxiety.

Insecurity is an attack on who you are and your value as a daughter of Christ and a wife. Every time you compare yourself to another woman, you're cooperating with insecurity's plan to play you: "You're too . . . not enough . . . she has more . . . your husband wants what she has . . . You didn't . . ." Like fear, insecurity looks for a soft spot, drills down, and parks there.

Until you kick it out.

Here's the deal: you will never overcome a trigger by passively sitting there and allowing it to have its way with you. You have to be aware of what's going on, step back, and look honestly at the situation, apply wisdom and truth, take up your God-given weapons when needed, use them effectively, and give yourself the space to recover if the situation calls for it (e.g., if you're hurting).

God isn't going to take your battles away from you, just as He isn't going to take your husband's sexual sin away. You both have your part to play if you want to be an overcomer. Many Christians waste their breath when they ask God to take away their trials. He takes us through them, not out. God uses our trials to burn off fear and pride, forge new faith, rebuild character, and reveal Himself to those who love Him.

Let's enhance your perspective.

First, you aren't a perfect ten when it comes to your body. Neither are the other women you're comparing yourself to. There is no such thing as a perfect woman, just as there is no perfect man. Men look up to the Arnold Schwarzenegger of the '70s and '80s as the standard for the body they want, but what does Arnold look like today? Just another old man.

Those women you're comparing yourself to have the same black sin nature you do. They may look good for the moment, but under the hood—which is what counts and determines whether a relationship will make it over the long haul—they're no better than you are, especially not in God's eyes.

75

The vast majority of those women want nothing to do with your husband. They'd laugh at him if he approached them. Many would be sickened when they found out he was married. Those twenty-year-olds? How many really want an older guy, especially if he's in his forties, fifties, or sixties?

Your husband has a sin problem with lust. Even if you were a perfect ten, it would never resolve your husband's porn problem because lust is never satisfied and always wants "more and better."

Your husband is blinded to your incredible worth as his God-given wife. Another woman will never satisfy him—you are the only woman who can satisfy your husband sexually. I had sex with other women before I married Michelle, and there was always a sense that something was missing afterward. When I'm referring to sexual satisfaction, I mean the entire package: physically, emotionally, and spiritually. You alone have the God-given gift to satisfy your husband completely when it comes to sex.

Porn will never satisfy your husband. It's just pictures; it's impossible for porn to satisfy a man in any way. I've never had a guy tell me they had a great time masturbating to porn, but have heard many stories of the incredible shame, guilt, and emptiness that torment them afterward.

If you're comparing yourself to porn, you're comparing yourself to something your husband hates. He loathes himself when he does it and it's destroying his life. You're comparing yourself to the image on the paper or screen that Satan uses to hook him. When men come out of the fog, they realize how insane it was that they opted for porn when they could have had great, satisfying sex with their wives.

Satan uses insecurity as a trap to compel you to compare yourself to others so he can distract you from your God-given identity as a beloved daughter of Christ. When insecurity strikes, you have to drive your stake in the ground, remember the truths I've mentioned above, and stand on who you are.

A woman who stands in her God-given, blood-bought identity as a daughter of Christ is not a victim. She doesn't lie down and allow insecurity to own her. She is a Spirit-filled woman with all the power and blessings of the living God available to her. She can do all things through Christ (Philippians 4:13). She is blessed and of extreme value to God and her husband.

When you're triggered, it's important that you remember to separate your husband's sexual sin from who you are. Never allow his sin to define you.

Let's look at fear. When your husband sinned against you, the trust in your marriage was shattered and now lies in pieces. Maybe you've been sifting through the rubble, frantically looking for something that will give you hope. Today, if there isn't much there, putting all of your hope in these broken pieces will drive you mad because your husband is a work-in-progress and your marriage is in the rebuilding process.

If you want to overcome fear, you have to go back to God and make your relationship with Him the bedrock of your trust and hope:

*"Do not fear, for I am with you; do not anxiously look about you, for I am your God. I will strengthen you, surely I will help you, surely I will uphold you with My righteous right hand."*
—Isaiah 41:10

If you and your husband are in the early stage of recovery and fear hits, and your first line of defense is to fight with statements like, "He won't do that again . . . he wouldn't hurt me again . . . he promised . . ." often, the enemy and your own fears will counter with, "Really? How do you know? He's fallen many times and made promises before. What makes today different?" Then the downward spiral begins.

Instead, go to God first: "Lord, I'm getting hit with fear. You said to trust you with all of my heart and not rely on my own understanding (Proverbs 3:5). Here I am, God. I'm putting my husband and what he does in your hands. I can't control what he does. Please show me what I should do next. Please give me the wisdom you promised when I ask for it (James 1:5). You are my rock. Please calm the storm of my emotions and help me to rest in you."

When a trigger hits, turn your focus away from it, focus on the Lord, openly share what you're going through, and invite Him into the battle. Then wait for His answer.

I call this turn and connect, and you can apply it to any temptation or trigger. We don't overcome our battles by using our weak flesh to wrestle with our flesh or emotions. Instead, we turn away from the adversary, connect with God and all of His endless power and grace, and invite Him into the battle to fill in the gaps and help us overcome.

*Turn away my eyes from looking at vanity, and revive me in Your ways*
—Psalm 119:37

*Do not be wise in your own eyes; Fear the LORD and turn away from evil.*
—Proverbs 3:7

*Turn to me and be saved, all the ends of the earth; For I am God, and there is no other.*
—Isaiah 45:22

Turning to God is an act of faith that counters fear. It takes all of the pressure off you to figure out the situation or what to do, and moves your heart and mind toward alignment with His.

As you connect with the Lord, He might speak to you, bring a verse to your mind, calm your spirit, encourage you to wait on Him, or give you a sense of what He wants you to do. He cares for you and wants you to invite Him into your fears, pain, and concern (I Peter 5:7).

Focusing on the trigger and obsessing gives it more power. Turning to God and focusing on Him weakens that which we're struggling with and cuts it down to size.

Some battles last longer than others. There are times when I'm wrestling with temptation and need to keep going to God for hours. Don't throw your hands up because you turned to God once and are still feeling overwhelmed. It will take time to build up your spiritual and emotional muscles, especially if you've been allowing the four triggers to have their way with you.

Later, as your husband recovers and trust is rebuilt, you can bring him into your resistance to fear: "My husband has not acted out for (X period of time), he's been treating me differently, and I have every reason to trust him again. Until my husband gives me a reason not to trust him, I will not fear, even if he slips. I know God is with us and will help us."

Let's move into what to do with your pain. A wounded person can't run as fast as a healthy one. They need to slow down and take care of themselves by cleaning their wounds, changing the dressings, and being careful to avoid re-injury.

When you're hurting, what is the best medicine for you? Everyone is wired differently so the answer isn't the same for everyone, but here is a list of care items for you to choose from:

Silence and solitude.

Worship music.

If you're with your husband and the pain is overwhelming you, you can ask him to pray for you, or tell him you need time alone, and excuse yourself.

Avoid situations, such as social gatherings, that will be too much of a drain on you.

Lighten your load. Remove things from your schedule that are expendable or unnecessary for the moment.

Slow down your pace of life. Wounded people are prone to hurt themselves if they move too fast.

Call a safe friend and ask them to pray for you.

Meet with a friend for coffee or a meal.

Do something you enjoy. Take a bath or go to a movie.

Spend time in God's word, especially the Psalms.

Prayer.



Another way to protect your heart from reinjury is to dole out trust to your husband slowly. Don't put all of your heart out there until he's made it safe for you to do so.

You don't owe him your heart, especially the vulnerable places; it's okay to wait until he's shown you he's a safe person and can be trusted.

Taking an all-or-nothing approach can get you hurt. This is a rebuilding process that takes time. If your husband is refusing to get help, being completely vulnerable will open your wound. Use wisdom and protect your heart.

Today, if Michelle and I were to see Dutch and her pain was triggered, I would ask her what she needed in the moment. I would have focused on listening. If a bath would have helped, I would have encouraged it.

When pain arises, ask God to reveal the best course of action you could take that would be a balm for your heart.

As the Master Physician, He knows best what would minister to you in the moment.

Whenever you're hit with fear, insecurity, anger, or pain, step back. Don't jump into the pool of your emotions. Look at what you're going through, get perspective on the bigger picture, and line it up with the truth as shown in God's word. Then turn and connect.

# NOTES

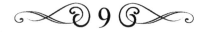

## You Are Jael

*Now Sisera fled away on foot to the tent of Jael the wife
of Heber the Kenite, for there was peace between Jabin
the king of Hazor and the house of Heber the Kenite.
Jael went out to meet Sisera, and said to him, "Turn
aside, my master, turn aside to me!
Do not be afraid." And he turned aside to her into the
tent, and she covered him with a rug.
He said to her, "Please give me a little water to drink,
for I am thirsty." So she opened a bottle of milk and gave
him a drink; then she covered him. He said to her,
"Stand in the doorway of the tent, and it shall be if
anyone comes and inquires of you, and says, 'Is there
anyone here?' that you shall say, 'No.'"
But Jael, Heber's wife, took a tent peg and seized a
hammer in her hand, and went secretly to him and drove
the peg into his temple, and it went through into the
ground; for he was sound asleep and exhausted.
So he died.*
—Judges 4:17–21

You, your husband, and your family are at war with the spiritual forces of darkness. Satan comes to "steal, kill and destroy" (John 10:10).

If he can't drive your marriage to divorce, he'll work to keep it crippled. If your husband recovers from sexual sin, the enemy will focus on keeping you trapped in pain, bitterness, and discouragement, just as he will attack your husband with lust.

It's not just the husband and wife he's after. Many men were exposed to porn by their fathers; some of those dads were pastors. When a boy or girl gets their first exposure to porn from Dad, it can have a debilitating effect on their belief in God and what sex is about.

The adversary is after more than a broken family. If the husband falls hard and long enough into sexual sin, the enemy tells him God doesn't hear his prayers and freedom is hopeless, so he might as well give up and walk away from God.

The enemy attacks you with fear and anxiety, does all he can to fan your anger into rage, and then works to harden your heart. If you spiral so deeply into discouragement that you lose hope, or your heart goes cold, he will try to convince you that God has abandoned you so you might as well walk away from Him.

Many of today's movies portray men as the only ones who do the fighting; women are weak damsels in distress. Feminists come off as semi-masculine anger-machines who are out to tear God's plan for marriage apart. Neither of these align with Scripture.

Look at how Jael handled the battle with Sisera in

Judges 4. She didn't scream at Sisera or charge him like an Amazon. She didn't cower in fear, run, or hide. She had her emotions under control in what must have been a frightening situation. Sisera was a warrior who could have raped and killed her.

She approached Sisera calmly and invited him into her tent. He would have barged in anyway so she took the initiative and engaged him on her terms. Jael won the battle with wisdom, courage, waiting for the right moment, and taking brutal action.

Though you may not feel like it, you are Jael, beloved daughter of the living God, empowered with the Holy Spirit, given every blessing in heaven (Ephesians 1:3), and armed with powerful spiritual weapons that destroy strongholds (II Corinthians 10:4) and change lives. You have access to the same everlasting well of wisdom and power that Jael did, even more so because you're indwelt by the Holy Spirit.

Maybe you're thinking, "None of this comes close to how I feel today. I'm a mess. My heart is torn up, my husband is abusive, my faith is weak, and I have no idea what I'm doing. What you just wrote about me being Jael sounds unreal—how can it be true for me? I've given in to fear, anxiety, anger, and discouragement so many times that I don't know how to fight."

Training camp for spiritual warrior-ettes begins now.

First, if you put all of your focus on your emotions, the chances are high you will lose and give in to fear, anger, or whatever is tormenting you. You may not feel strong, but how you feel is irrelevant to being an overcomer. The key is to take the right actions and use the weapons God has placed at your disposal, regardless of how you feel.

In 2009, I was in an intense trial that had been going on for three years. Fear and anxiety had been overwhelming me to the point of panic attacks. I spent a lot of time with doctors and made several visits to the emergency room. None of the medications they gave me worked; in fact, they made it worse.

I went to the church for answers, even some who had experience with spiritual warfare, with the same results. Every time I turned to people for help, it blew up in my face.

As I later understood, a big part of my problem was that I had been putting all of my hope in people for help and answers. God allowed everything they did to fail in order to force me to make Him my only hope. Once we allow fear to drive us—which is what I had been doing—we're apt to take our eyes off God and put our hope in what can be seen. When you're in a spiritual battle, that which is in the physical realm cannot overcome the forces in the spiritual realm through physical means.

I want to make a disclaimer here that not every problem is spiritual. There are times when we need healing emotionally (which we'll get into later in this book) or when our body chemistry is off and medication is required. If you've been through a lot of stress for an extended period, your serotonin or adrenal levels may be so off that you need the help of medication, at least temporarily. There's nothing wrong with medication in the proper context. In my case, the Lord was showing me that turning to man for help wasn't going to work.

One morning in November 2009, as I was alone in my office, a force of evil filled the room with such intensity that I felt it physically. There was a heavy sense of pressure in the room, as if I were being squeezed in a vise of fear.

Up to that time, when I'd been hit with overwhelming fear or a panic attack, I'd run to man for help. It dawned on me that morning that if I ran again, I would give the force in the room what it wanted: to give in to fear again and allow it to drive me, and I would be in a far worse place than before.

I didn't know what to do. Fighting a demonic force that strong wasn't anything I had experience with, and I was certainly no expert in spiritual warfare. I cried out to God and told Him if He wanted my life, He could have it.

He didn't take it. As the pressure mounted, I grabbed a Bible, opened it to the Psalms, and started praying the verses. I put all of my hope in God and held on for life; He was all I had.

After fifteen minutes of praying through the Psalms, the evil presence began to fade. A tiny seed of faith, God, and His word were enough to provide the breakthrough. Not once during the battle did I feel brave, like I knew what I was doing, or strong. I had no idea if I was going to pull through and what that even looked like. Relief came after the battle had been won.

Fast-forward three years. It's 2012, and I'm in the second day of a five-day Daniel fast. I'm in much better shape; the anxiety and panic attacks have been gone since 2009, my faith is strong, and my belief in who I am in Christ is growing.

From the time I woke up that morning, my mind was assaulted with dark thoughts. I can usually tell when I'm getting hit with a spiritual attack versus a set of random thoughts fluttering through my mind because the thoughts are evil and keep coming. There is a sense I'm being wailed on.

Which is what happened that morning. I prayed through Scripture like I did in 2009, but this time, the assault kept coming. As I drove on the way to the office, I got angry and at the top of my voice, I shouted, "In the name of Jesus Christ, I who am a citizen of heaven, seated with Christ in heaven, command any evil spirits that are messing with me in any way to stop, leave my presence, and go where Jesus sends you to go!"

Instant silence. The assault was over. This time, I needed to take up my authority in Christ to overcome.

I shared these stories to provide a picture of the intensity of the battles you will face and what being victorious looks like. Most of you may not encounter battles that fierce, but the fight will still be difficult.

Not long ago, I had an appointment scheduled to counsel a wife over the phone who needed help coping with her husband's sexual sin. When we got on the phone, she told me she'd experienced a sharp stab of fear that morning that she couldn't explain. Her day had been going fine and she hadn't been thinking about anything prior to that moment that could have caused it. She said she realized it was an attack of the enemy, probably to keep her from the call.

In both of my stories, I was alone; so was Jael when she encountered Sisera. While there may have been someone praying for me, I had to stand up and fight. God is enough to get you through every battle, temptation, and trigger. He is always there to help you (Hebrews 13:5).

Each battle is different; there is no cookie-cutter approach that works every time. Christmas morning of 2009, I was being assaulted again with dark thoughts. My wife and four kids were around me. Bringing them into my situation didn't feel right; I didn't want them thinking I was crazy. I silently asked the Lord what to do, and the word praise came to my mind. In my heart, I began praising God; within minutes, I had peace. Bring God into every battle, and ask Him what to do.

The word of God is another weapon in your arsenal. Let's say you're hit with a barrage of fear-thoughts that your husband might be viewing porn. You bring the Lord into battle in prayer, then go back to a verse that you can stand on in His word, such as Isaiah 41:10 or Deuteronomy 31:6. Say the verse aloud if you want to. God is with you and you will never be alone. He is with you in this temptation to give in to fear and He will see you through. Then go to Proverbs 3:5–6: "Trust in the LORD with all your heart and do not lean on your own understanding. In all your ways acknowledge Him, and He will make your paths straight."

In obedience to Proverbs 3:5–6, you release your husband and his recovery to the Lord. When you're able to do what God's word says and not just say the verses, victory will come quicker, which leads us back to:

Obedience. There may be times when God is calling you to take an action step. If, after praying and getting the counsel of a trusted, safe friend, you feel there's something you believe the Lord is calling you to do, no matter how hard it is, proceed. I've never regretted obeying God, even when He asked me to do something that took me out of my comfort zone and sounded crazy to others.

There have been several instances when I asked my Christian friends for their feedback on what I thought God wanted me to do and they disagreed with me; yet the more I prayed, the more I was convicted that I had to proceed. In the end, doing what I believed God was calling me to do turned out to be the right move. If Abraham had sought the counsel of others when the Lord told him to sacrifice Isaac, I bet all of them would have said Abraham was nuts. If you know God is calling you to obey in an area, move forward—just make sure your heart is aligned with His and you know you've clearly heard from Him and it's not your flesh or the enemy.

You will be at war until the day you die. This doesn't mean you'll be fighting twenty-four-seven, but there will be times when you get hit and need to go at it. Passivity and apathy will keep you bound in defeat. If I would have done nothing that morning in 2009 in my office, the battle would have intensified to the point where I had a panic attack, then who knows what might have happened. If you allow fear or rage to wash over you unchecked, it will keep going until it sends you over the edge, or you ram a spiritual stake through its head.

Prayer is your most powerful weapon. I believe that prayer alone is enough to carry me through every temptation. The most powerful spiritual battle in history may have been at the Garden of Gethsemane, when Jesus wrestled with the pull to walk away from the cross.

These were His instructions to His disciples for the battle ahead:

> *And He came to the disciples and found them sleeping, and said to Peter, "So, you men could not keep watch with Me for one hour? Keep watching and praying that you may not enter into temptation; the spirit is willing, but the flesh is weak."*
> —Matthew 26:40–41

The only weapon He gave them was prayer. While there will be times when you might need to take up your authority in Christ or pray though God's word, it's in prayer where the Lord will reveal the next step to you. My pastor has said that "Satan laughs when we have a Bible study, but he trembles when we pray." As we send prayer upward, God responds with His answer.

Pray when you wake up, during the day, when you get hit with trials, and before you go to bed at night. A prayerless Christian is powerless, just as a prayer-saturated believer is strong in the Spirit.

Many Christians have a weak to nonexistent prayer life; so do many churches (when is the last time your church spent twenty minutes or more in prayer on a Sunday morning?). Prayer takes effort, focus, and time. Firing off "God bless me" is about self and checking off a box, not God. Effective prayer focuses on the Lord, not the self or its desires. It involves listening as well as talking—an exchange that can be marked by silence as well as praise, petition, and thanksgiving.

There will be battles when you have to press in and keep praying until there is a breakthrough. I've heard Christians complain that "I prayed, and God didn't answer me." This is a one-and-done approach. They get hit with temptation, offer one weak prayer, then cave. That's not prevailing prayer, which is to keep going until the battle is won. If someone came at your kids and you shot the attacker once but they kept coming, you would keep firing until they dropped. It's the same with prayer.

The answer to prayer doesn't always come at once. While there have been instances when God spoke immediately to me, relief or answers sometimes arrived hours or days later. Be sensitive to the Spirit's leading. He might want you to pray once or twice, then wait for Him to come through.

Prayer plays a critical role in the healing of your marriage. Pray with your husband once daily, no matter what you're going through. Bring God into your relationship consistently. There have been instances when Michelle and I felt distant from each other, but after we prayed the gap closed.

Even though you may feel like your husband is your enemy because he's hurt you, he's not your enemy. Satan is. The Devil wants to keep you and your husband fighting against each other instead of with each other against him. Remember who your true enemy is. If your husband is raging or blaming you, it's because he's spiritually blind. Remove the blinders, and he will instantly see that you're the most precious gift God has given him, next to his salvation.

In your solo moments with the Lord, pray for your

husband every day. I value my wife's prayers above all others, because she sees my weaknesses and knows what I need at a deep level. In the same way, you are your husband's most valuable intercessor.

Saturate your mind in God's word daily. The best way to counter Satan's lies is with the truth, which you can't do if you don't know it. God's word will shape your character, give light to your decisions, strengthen your faith, and give you the wisdom to know how to stand in the truth.

As you notch victories in your belt, store what God has taught you and how He's brought you through in your faith arsenal. Remembrance of God's faithfulness in tough times is a faith-builder. Since He's helped you before, He will do so again; His character doesn't change. When the enemy slings the stones of doubt at you, hold on to the anchors of faithfulness from your victories of the past.

You are not a victim. Satan has tried to convince you that you are weak and helpless, without hope, and alone. These are all lies. You can do all things through Christ who strengthens you (Philippians 4:13). Just as I had more weapons at my disposal than I knew that morning in my office in 2009, so do you. You just needed to be made aware of all that God has given you and how to use it.

Always stand firm on who you are: you are Jael, beloved daughter of God; a woman of uncommon, Holy Spirit-fired strength, who can face any foe and come through victorious, because greater is He who is in you than He who is in the world (I John 4:4). You are given

Christ's authority, and armed with everything you need to overcome the enemy. No weapon formed against you shall prosper (Isaiah 54:17).

I suggest that you read through the book of Ephesians. The first two chapters provide insight into your authority in Christ and what God has done for you. Ephesians 6 deals with spiritual warfare.

*Finally, be strong in the Lord and in the strength of His might. Put on the full armor of God, so that you will be able to stand firm against the schemes of the devil. For our struggle is not against flesh and blood, but against the rulers, against the powers, against the world forces of this darkness, against the spiritual forces of wickedness in the heavenly places. Therefore, take up the full armor of God, so that you will be able to resist in the evil day, and having done everything, to stand firm.*
—Ephesians 6:10–13

# NOTES

## 10

### Coping the Right Way

*I've been coping with my husband's porn use with emotional eating and am seeing a counselor for help. We're having a family gathering later today; I need prayer that our sometimes awkward relationships won't ruin it. Although my husband slipped again last week, he's making progress. Prior to that time, he'd achieved eight weeks of not acting out, which is a big deal for him.*

We bring our coping methods for dealing with trials into our marriage. Most were learned from our parents. We watched how they related to each other and reacted to stressful situations, and internalized their ways. It would be nice if we could filter their bad coping mechanisms and retain the good, but, as our spouse will attest, that didn't happen.

Our character strengths and flaws play a part. Extroverts deal with suffering differently than introverts; extroverts may be more confrontational, while the introvert prefers to withdraw in their shell.

Let's examine healthy and unhealthy coping methods for the wife of a sex addict.

**Bad:** Revenge.

Pursuing an affair or doing something to hurt your husband won't move your marriage toward healing. Revenge feeds anger and inflates pride; it will compound his sin with your own. Don't go there. The antidote to revenge is release: surrendering your husband and his sins to God and allowing the Lord to be his judge.

If you've been playing with fire by flirting with another man, whether in person or online, cut off all contact now. Run away as fast as you can, and don't look back.

*Never take your own revenge, beloved, but leave room for the wrath of God, for it is written, "VENGEANCE IS MINE, I WILL REPAY,"*
*says the Lord.*
—Romans 12:19

**Good:** Expressing your heart in a healthy way.

Stuffing your emotions is like taking dynamite and putting it in a sealed, fully heated oven. When it blows, everyone's going to get hit.

It's important that you communicate your pain, how he's hurt you, the anger, disappointment, and all that you're going through to your husband. This is part of the process of rebuilding your relationship. He needs to understand how he's hurt you so he can do his part to rebuild the marriage, which includes listening and caring for you.

While you need to express your hurt and anger, it's just as important that he is able to receive what you've shared. Raging, screaming, insults, a flow of four-letter words, or passive-aggressive comments ("No, I'm fine, you jerk!") will push his fight-or-flight hot button and start a nuclear war that no one wins.

If, in conflict, you default to "Ready, Fire, Aim, oops, shouldn't have said that," work at praying and thinking about the best way to talk to your husband before you approach him. If your anger is boiling, wait. Talk it through with a safe friend, or take a walk to take the edge off. Then approach your husband.

Sticking with the facts and staying focused can help you avoid stepping on an emotional land mine. Here's an example of speaking the truth in a way that has a better chance of getting through: in a reasonably calm voice, "I'm angry and frustrated that you lied again about using porn. It's impossible for us to rebuild our marriage without trust. I need complete honesty. If you're not able to give me that, we're going to have to discuss alternative living arrangements. I love you. Please tell me how I can help you."

Here's the wrong way: "You *@#! Jerk! You #!@% lied to me again! You're nothing but a lying pervert who wouldn't know the truth from a hole in the ground! When are you going to start telling me the truth, you lowlife hypocrite!?"

A while ago, my wife and I were having an argument

over something insignificant. Later, with no prompting from me, she walked outside in the cold and knocked the snow off the windshield of my car. Michelle didn't know I was watching; her kindness melted my heart with conviction. Here she was, serving me, and I did nothing to deserve it. I felt like a complete idiot for being mad at her over a nonessential issue.

Your purity, humility, and quiet strength have immense convicting power. Even if your husband has a hard heart or is not in a place where he gets it, I can assure you that your kindness will eventually work its way through the cracks in his heart.

*Therefore, laying aside falsehood, SPEAK TRUTH EACH ONE of you WITH HIS NEIGHBOR, for we are members of one another. BE ANGRY, AND yet DO NOT SIN; do not let the sun go down on your anger, and do not give the devil an opportunity.*
*—Ephesians 4:25–27*

*In the same way, you wives, be submissive to your own husbands so that even if any of them are disobedient to the word, they may be won without a word by the behavior of their wives*
*—I Peter 3:1*

**Bad:** Withdrawing for an extended period of time.

When the most important person in our life deeply wounds us, withdrawing into a protective shell is a natural response. We withdraw to protect ourselves, assess what happened, question why, deal with shock, sort out emotions, and examine our next move. All good things.

But withdrawing for weeks or months can be deadly for your marriage. When one spouse covers up for a long time, the other may respond in kind. Frustration mounts, hearts harden, and apathy sinks in.

The healing process can't begin without frank discussions of the tough topics; consistent, open communication is vital.

Perhaps you're dreading the conversations you know need to take place but have had enough pain and don't want to get hurt again. The only way out is through; wounds heal after they're exposed and cleaned. Hiding an injury makes it fester; given enough time, it becomes infected.

**Bad:** Allowing the wrong people to poison your heart.

We looked at this in chapter five. If your "friends," who have their own baggage, are fueling your anger instead of calming it, adding more shame instead of dissolving it, or if all you hear from them is "divorce the dirty blank-blank," find new friends. The same for counselors and pastors.

**Good:** Talking and praying with one safe person or a group at least once a week. More is better.

This is critical to your healing and sanity. You need

other safe Christian women who will listen, encourage, challenge, and pray for you.

**Bad:** Turning to food, alcohol, or drugs for comfort.

Turning to food, alcohol, or drugs for comfort will compound the pain in your marriage with more guilt, shame, and confusion.

No church will justify drugs or alcohol, but many Christians wink at comfort foods. Church-sponsored events are notorious for offering nutritional standouts such as doughnuts and cookies. While an occasional, small portion of desserts is okay, pounding down a bag of Oreos is as effective at soothing your pain as your husband's porn habit.

You'll also feel lousy afterward.

Keep going, and you'll gain weight and experience health problems. Instead:

**Good:** Take care of yourself.

What you're going through is traumatic. You need adequate rest, exercise, and good nutrition to counter the stress. Embrace healthy proteins like chicken and fish, good carbs such as vegetables, healthy grains (oatmeal), and fruits, and healthy fats like avocados, seeds, coconut oil, and nuts. Reduce or stay away from anything processed, sodas, or processed sugars. Getting amped on caffeine weakens your immune system. Chamomile tea is a calming alternative.

Give yourself the space and time you need to do the

things that bring rest, peace, and enjoyment. Wrapping yourself around your problems "until they're fixed" to the exclusion of everything else will burn you out. Take baths, meet with a friend for coffee or a meal, go to a movie, or spend time with crafts or hobbies. Get out of the house. You might consider going away for weekend with a lady friend.

If you have kids and your husband won't watch them, ask a friend. Or take them with you and meet a friend who has children so they can play while you have a little downtime.

Taking care of yourself is an important part of your healing process—don't neglect it. Some of you may have a hard time with this because the idea of doing something fun, just for you, isn't "spiritual." You're not a machine—you're a human being with limits and weaknesses. Push yourself too hard, and you'll be a candidate for burnout and anxiety attacks.

You need fun and rest to recharge your batteries and melt away the stress.

*One hand full of rest is better than two fists full of labor and striving after wind.*
—Ecclesiastes 4:6

**Good:** Thin out your schedule.

This is the wrong time to ramp up ministry or other projects. Wounded people need to slow down until they've had time to heal. Think of yourself as a marathon runner with a torn Achilles' heel: there's no way you'd consider entering a race until your foot could stand up to the demands of competition.

If your schedule is packed, at least temporarily, say no, resign from, or take a leave of absence from the nonessentials.

**Bad:** Going on a spending spree.

It's not rare for couples to be in financial straits because the husband has put them in debt spending money on his sexual sin.

Don't dig the hole deeper by running up another credit card (or two or three). Be the voice of sanity and restraint in your marriage and keep your expenses in line with your income. If you need to, cut up your credit cards. Use debit cards only.

Racking up debt will crank up the pressure in your marriage another notch. You don't need that right now.

**Good:** Worship.

Sometimes when I'm going through a difficult time, I'll get alone, turn on praise music, and worship the Lord.

My Bible is closed, the smartphone is off, and my sole desire is to draw near to the Lord. Taking our focus off our problems and resetting it on Him is how we find rest and peace in the midst of insanity.

God ministers to us in these moments; we exchange our grief and sorrow for His kindness and love.

As you worship, feel free to pour your heart out to Him, as a hurting daughter to her Father.

# COPING THE RIGHT WAY

*Trust in Him at all times, O people; Pour out your heart before Him; God is a refuge for us.*
—Psalm 62:8

*Draw near to God and He will draw near to you.*
—James 4:8

# NOTES

# 11

## The Eight Elements of Rebuilding Trust

*I just found out my husband has been using porn. Over time, he's became distant; he doesn't even kiss me good night anymore. I've dreamed of having a beautiful marriage where my husband loves me like Jesus loves the church, but our relationship is far from that. I've complained about our lack of sex many times, but he hasn't changed. This year has been horrible; I feel so lonely. I'm not eating right or sleeping well, and am struggling with anxiety. Having kids has changed my body; I'll never be one of those women he lusts over. I trusted my husband to protect my heart. Did he ever care?*

Trust is the cornerstone of marriage; relationships die without it.

The husband who is incapable of consistent honesty and accountability cannot give his wife a reason to trust him. Without the security that comes from a relationship built on trust, their marriage cannot be rebuilt.

On the other hand, a man who answers his wife's

questions truthfully, no matter how difficult they may be, is worthy of her trust. Honest men show their wives that their relationship means more to them than their pride, which is often the first hindrance to transparency. Fear and shame take second and third. Although a man of integrity is fatally flawed and makes mistakes, he is willing to own up to them. He doesn't wear a mask or fake the Christian life.

After a wife has discovered her husband has been lying and deceiving her for years, even decades, what does the process of rebuilding trust look like? Can she trust him again?

Years ago, I went to a federal prison for training to minister to inmates. The instructor told us that some prisoners are out to manipulate those from the outside into doing something for them, such as smuggling or making contact with one of their friends for illicit purposes.

He told us that violent criminals aren't the hardest to trust—the sex offenders are. When it comes to deceit, sex offenders are the professionals. Lie detector tests are often included in their rehabilitation programs to determine if they can be trusted.

As we discussed in chapter two, most men get hooked on porn or other forms of sexual sin as a teen, then spend years hiding, lying, and deceiving, well into their marriage. Dishonesty is woven into their character.

I don't write this to discourage you, but to help you understand what you might be dealing with. The normal rules that govern a healthy relationship where both sides can be trusted don't apply here.

Not all men are in this deep when it comes to dishonesty. Some are so desperate and broken they'll do anything to heal their marriage. Honesty and accountability are easier for them because they've had enough pain, are sick of the double life, and don't want to keep hurting their spouse.

Let's swing the pendulum and examine both sides to understand the men who struggle with dishonesty. To the left are those who are paralyzed by fear and shame. Telling the truth to these men is terrifying because of the fear of rejection and how their spouse will respond. They've rarely crawled out of their shame-hole. Exposing the depths of their sin and brokenness may be difficult because their loved ones (usually Mom or Dad) never accepted them, faults and all. This makes honesty an intimidating mountain for them to face. Deep down, they want to stop lying and hiding, but fear and shame have such a tight grip on them that they're in bondage. The good news is that these guys can recover and heal with acceptance, love, and facing their fears.

Then there are those on the opposite side of the pendulum. Their hearts are rock-hard. While honesty sounds nice, they won't give up their pride. They'll manipulate, blame, coerce, lie, and justify to get what they want. These men are the professional posers, the liars who my instructor in prison was referring to. They are found at every level of the church, including pastors. Sadly, these men need industrial-strength consequences to break them before they'll face their sin.

The rebuilding of trust requires time, not a one-time event. As Hansel and Gretel left small pebbles on the path so they could find their way home, so you will dole out small nuggets of trust to your husband as he earns them. Don't give him the whole loaf at once; he must earn it back by taking consistent actions over an extended period of time, just as he did when you were dating.

To gauge whether you can believe your husband and dole out a nugget of trust, consider the following eight elements. One won't provide enough information for a solid judgment call—you'll need all eight.

1. The first element determines how far you can open the door of trust. Where is his heart? Which of the three men at the beginning of this chapter do you see him as? Broken with a soft heart, fearful and in bondage to lying yet willing to change, or with a heart of stone?

If he has a hard heart, you have no reason to trust him; he isn't willing to change and/or doesn't want to give up sexual sin. I wouldn't open the door of trust more than a hairline crack for a guy like this.

If his character is laced with deception and fear, yet he's willing to change, you can open the door of trust a bit, maybe six inches. This will give both of you hope and a starting place to work from. He's not granted wide-open access to your heart; that comes later after he changes.

If he's like the first man who's willing to do whatever it takes to heal your marriage, with a broken and soft heart, you can open the door around a foot. This is telling him, "I'm willing to start by giving you several nuggets of my trust, which are precious to me. Let's see what happens." He gets a piece of your heart, and you're letting light and grace in your relationship. He doesn't have wide-open access yet, but could if he keeps changing.

The door represents protection for your heart; how vulnerable you will be. Trust is not just about honesty; as trust grows you feel more secure, and as you feel more secure, you can be vulnerable with your husband and give him more of you. In each of the three cases you're protecting your heart. The level of protection is determined by how much the door is closed. You open the door more as they earn your trust by how well they're doing with these eight elements.

2. Gauge if your husband is taking the five action steps that were described in chapter six on a consistent basis. You must give your husband's actions far more weight than his words; talk doesn't move the scale. If he isn't taking the action steps, close the door. If he says, "I can do this on my own"; "I don't need help"; or "I will get help tomorrow," but doesn't follow through, it's all smoke and mirrors and he's playing you.

If he's going to a group and or/meeting with an accountability partner at least once a week and taking the other action steps, and has been doing it every week without stopping for at least several months, you have a reason to consider opening the door a little more.

Note that I said you can consider opening the door; you're never obligated to grant him a nugget of trust. You don't owe him; he's in your debt. That doesn't mean you should lord it over him and set the bar unreasonably high (stay away from revenge mode), but that you should use discretion and wisdom for every nugget of trust you dole out, apart from external pressure from him. Every piece of trust should come freely from your heart, not under pressure or false guilt.

3. Ask your husband for a complete account of his sexual history. It all needs to come out—the sooner, the better. You don't want him taking the Hansel and Gretel approach with you where he throws you a few truth crumbs over weeks or months. The "tell it all as we go" approach scrapes your wounds and sets the rebuilding process back.

Ask him the hard questions: When did he start acting out sexually, and how (porn, prostitutes, promiscuity, affairs, stripper bars)? How often has he acted out since then, with whom, and/or how? When was the last time he binged?

Examine his response. Is he answering every one of your questions without blowing up or getting defensive? For example, if you ask your husband, "When was the last time you masturbated to porn?" and he deflects or gets angry, that doesn't signal he's changed enough for you to open the door. It's also possible he may not have acted out but is still foundering in fear or Me mode. Don't assume he's viewed porn—wait until you know the truth.

If he answers your questions with humility, you have a reason to consider trusting him.

4. How is he treating you? Is he the same self-absorbed jerk he was before, or is he making genuine attempts to change? Is he kinder, more patient, and does he listen to you? Don't expect him to get it all together over night; he has a long process ahead of unwinding

selfishness and learning to love. If his parents were lousy role models when it came to caring for each other, he probably absorbed some of their faulty habits. You're looking for progress, not perfection.

Is he dating you? Is your sex life on the mend? Is he sharing his heart with you so that your relationship is about more than talking about recovery and family issues? Are you getting to know him?

5. Is he engaged at home? Does he help out, and is he spending time with your kids? If he was a workaholic, is he reducing his work hours so he can adjust his life to his God-given priorities, with you and your family at the top of the list?

6. Is he having fun with you and your kids? Is he laughing more? For many sex addicts, porn was their only fun. Laughter and cutting loose are positive signals that he's discovering life again.

7. How's he doing with overcoming sexual sin? If he's still binging every week but is honest with you and still going to groups, you can keep the door where it is, or close it a little. If he's slipping and no longer taking the action steps, close the door. If he's gaining traction and is beginning to walk in freedom, you have a reason to consider opening it.

8. Are you catching him in lies? If he lied to you recently but felt remorse and came to you and confessed, you might consider keeping the door where it is. But if you're catching him in lies, and especially if it's a pattern, the door stays closed until he changes. If he's been rigorously honest, you have reason to consider extending a nugget of trust to him.

"Since sex addicts are so good at lying, how do I know if he's telling me the truth?" you might ask.

Perhaps your husband was able to deceive you before because you trusted him completely. But now that you know the truth and your husband knows you know, it's going to be harder for him to look you in the eye and deceive you. He may be able to keep some things from you, but it won't last long and the truth will come out much sooner than before.

Women have a sixth sense when it comes to their husbands—they see right through them. If I'm in a bad place, Michelle knows after just one look at me. If she asks, "Is something wrong?" but I don't feel like talking about it and reply "Nothing," she'll give me the look that says, "Uh-huh, sure." Whether I want to talk or not, I know that she knows.

Learn to trust your gut. If something doesn't feel right, wait, watch, and ask again. If your husband is having a bad day, he'll eventually break out of it. If the pattern continues for days, it's a sign that something may be off and you need to press on.

Note that the eight elements are based on his actions and what they're showing you about your husband's character. If he's growing, his words will be reflected by consistent actions and the fruit of a changed heart, which translate into how he treats you.

*You will know them by their fruits. Grapes are not gathered from thorn bushes nor figs from thistles, are they? So every good tree bears good fruit, but the bad tree bears bad fruit. A good tree cannot produce bad*

*fruit, nor can a bad tree produce good fruit. Every tree that does not bear good fruit is cut down and thrown into the fire. So then, you will know them by their fruits.*
—Matthew 7:16–20

If fear is crawling up your spine, wait and pray before making a judgment call. You may need to step back and examine whether you're discerning that something isn't right in your husband, or if you're being driven by fear or paranoia. Fear drives with the sense of urgency that something must be done now. Wisdom prayerfully takes all of the facts into consideration before acting.

Which brings us back to God. Keep praying for wisdom and discernment as to whether you should release a nugget of trust to your husband. God will grant your request if you wait for the answer, just as He promised (James 1:5).

# NOTES

 12

## How You Can Help Him

*It's been almost two years since my husband's confession of porn addiction. With the exception of one slip, he's been pure the entire time. He's always been a great husband and I wouldn't say that we have a bad marriage. We've told very few people. He has an accountability partner, but I need another woman to talk to.*

Your husband needs help outside of your marriage with an accountability partner or support group, counseling, and other resources.

He also needs your help, desperately.

Whether he realizes it or not, your help will mean more to him and have more impact than anything anyone else does.

I've been in this ministry since 2000 and have seen God set many men free. He's allowed me to be a part of wives' healing and the restoration of marriages.

But if my wife isn't behind me or doesn't believe in what I'm doing, it means little to me. Michelle's love and acceptance have the most impact on my life, second only to God's. If I don't have her blessing on something I'm doing, my heart isn't in it. We're knit together as soulmates, lovers, and best friends. If our relationship isn't right, neither am I.

But, if Michelle is behind me, look out! I'll rock this thing.

Earlier this year, I went to Europe to speak on healing from porn in churches and other venues. While I got a lot of support from my friends and others who are in the ministry, one short text from my wife meant the most to me. She wrote, "Go and speak the truth." That was all I needed to light it up and go for it.

Your God-given role as your husband's wife is a game-changer. The influence you have on him, your advice, and especially, your love and acceptance, are powerful; many men would love to hear the words "I believe in you" from their wives.

The opposite is also true. If you shred him with criticism, or if he rarely hears words of love or encouragement, he'll feel crippled in your marriage. He may act tough on the outside, but inside, once you get past the walls, he wants to know you believe in him.

A friend of mine was a tough-as-nails colonel in the military (he's retired now); he led a regiment of two hundred tanks in battle in Iraq. Yet this battle-seasoned warrior told me, "I fear two people, God and my wife." This isn't because his wife was mean-spirited (I know her), but because of the profound impact she has on him.

Some men are dying in their marriages, not because they don't love their wives, but because their wives cut them down more than they build them up. "I can't do anything right so why try?" I've heard men say they don't know how to win with their wives because when they do A, she criticizes him for B, or asks when C will get done.

Treating your husband poorly doesn't justify what he did or heal your pain. No wife gets it right all of the time. The idea here is if you want to rebuild your marriage, you will need to come alongside your husband at some point and resume your role as his number-one fan.

Here's what that looks like:

1. Show him grace when he confesses his failures. Many men are terrified of how their wife will respond when they confess their sin to them, sexual or otherwise. I'm assuming that by now your husband has made a full confession of his sexual history to you and hopefully is making progress on the road to recovery. If he comes to you and confesses sin, work to respond in grace, just as Jesus does with you when you confess your sins to Him.

When a marriage is marked by grace and both spouses work to extend forgiveness as quickly as possible, their relationship strengthens, grows, and flourishes. To respond in grace and forgive quickly is to show your spouse that your love and commitment for them is far greater than their flaws and mistakes.

Even today, after being married since 1989, it's still hard (and embarrassing) for me to go to my wife and admit I said or did something wrong that upset her. Because she knows me so well, there is a fear she might get angry or use what I did against me later.

But, usually, when I go to her and apologize, she

says, "Okay," and it's over. She doesn't lecture me, say, "I told you so," or pull out the shame-and-blame gun.

Next to our relationship with God, the place where grace has the most impact is in marriage. In some ways, marriage reflects our relationship with the Lord. He sees every one of our weaknesses, sin, and failures; yet He accepts us with kindness and forgives immediately (I John 1:9). There is no retribution, condemnation, or requirement that we make up for our sin, which is impossible anyway.

When Michelle extends grace to me after I've confessed I've blown it, I'm released from fear and my love for her deepens.

2. Tell your husband how he can win. After I confessed my adultery to Michelle in 1991, I was desperate to know what I could do to heal our relationship. Tell your husband what you need from him. Expecting him to read your mind, discern your emotional state, and know what you want in the moment is a mistake that will build a wall of resentment between the two of you.

Perhaps your husband walks in the door and catches you when you're a volcano that's ready to blow. Or maybe you're in a fragile place, ready to crumble. Or you're wiped out from a day chasing screaming kids around the house.

If you need to talk and don't want him trying to fix you but want him to listen, say so. If you're overwhelmed or worn out and need space (or a hot bath), make it clear.

Men need black-and-white instructions; it's the way

we're wired. Occasionally, they need the help of a third party. When I'm working with a guy whose marriage is floundering, I'll ask him what his wife has been saying she wants from him. Many already know what their wife wants but are stuck in a rut. I point out that he already knows what to do—he just needs to do it. We then come up with an action plan for him to work on the following week.

Let's go a little deeper. When a man has been chasing porn for years, what often happens is he stops chasing his wife. The love in their relationship dies, as does their sex life. If this goes on long enough, he can get so deep into the fantasy world that he forgets what going after her is about.

Maybe reading this makes you angry; understandably so. A part of your relationship has been lost because of something that's not real and it feels foolish, if not insane, that you should have to tell your husband you want him to chase you.

Nevertheless, this chapter is about how you can help your husband, and the reality is that he's trying to fight his way out of the lust fog. Many men had lousy role models (or none at all) growing up for what loving a wife looks like. Then when they got married, they had nothing to bring to the marriage for making the relationship work. These men need their wives to help them by gently reminding them what will bless them.

Be specific. Is it dinner at a nice restaurant, a movie, a weekend away, notes under the pillow, flowers, lunch or coffee, or unexpected expressions of love that you'd like? Or all of the above, and he just needs to pick one?

Sex. For some marriages in the recovery process, this isn't an issue; all you have to do is look at your husband "that way," and it's on.

Others go through a drought for months, even years. I think eight years is the longest I'd heard a couple had gone without sex. That's the sign of a marriage on life support; sex is the bonding force in marriage. Without the glue, the two sides drift apart and become roommates.

If your marriage has been in the desert sexually, voice your desire to your husband. Sex is a vital part of marriage and is commanded in Scripture for the husband and wife:

*Stop depriving one another, except by agreement for a time, so that you may devote yourselves to prayer, and come together again so that Satan will not tempt you because of your lack of self-control.*
—I Corinthians 7:5

This doesn't mean you should be ready to go right after your husband discloses his sexual sin, but that sex needs to be reactivated in the marriage as you heal.

Some men are nervous about having sex with their wives after a long drought; shame and embarrassment over their sexual sin also factor in. Here again, grace, walking with him in his weakness, opens the door to restoration and healing.

Telling your husband what you want doesn't mean you should give him all the details. Give him the breathing room to be creative so he can come up with an idea that will surprise you.

3. Prayer. As we've discussed, the wife's prayers are the most coveted by her husband. Pray for him at least once a day. If you can, get one or two of your trusted friends (or support group) praying for your husband.

4. Patience. Don't expect him to get it all together overnight. If your husband has spent years immersing himself in lust, selfishness, and shame, it's going to take time (as in months or years, depending on his situation) for him to settle into living in freedom, break through the wall of self-absorption, and learn to love you in a meaningful way. Extend the same grace and patience to him you would need if you were struggling with besetting sin.

5. Words of encouragement. An embarrassed, shame-filled husband desperately needs this. When he can barely look you in the eye and hears you say, "I believe in you"; "Thank you for going to the support group. I know it's hard. I want you to know it means a lot to me"; or "Thank you for sharing your weaknesses with me. It's hard for me, yet I like that I'm getting to know you," it encourages him and builds him up. Over time, his self-perceived identity can transform from shameful husband who hurt his wife to the man she loves.

# NOTES

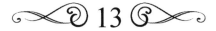

# 13

## What Has Been Exposed?

*Mike, I look forward to reading The Road to Grace and your workbook. I need healing; I lost a fifteen-year marriage due to my husband's porn addiction. I can't help but wonder how the wives of the men in our church's purity group are doing. Are they getting the help they need? How are they coping day to day?*

When you discovered your husband's sexual sin, his weaknesses were exposed. Assuming he stays on the path to healing and recovery, as time goes on, you will know your husband in a deep, intimate way. The real man will be revealed; his true, God-fueled strength and character. Like a master craftsman, God is fashioning a new man from the old.

At the same time, the suffering in your marriage has exposed you.

When an intense trial hits, the foundation on which our lives is built is revealed. If we were rooted in God, we may be shaken and broken, but there won't be a full-blown collapse.

If our lives were built on relationships with people, such as our spouse, when that relationship falters, we go with it.

Our priorities and coping mechanisms are forced to the surface in a crisis; so are any unresolved heart wounds. If we were distant from God, our faith may be in pieces.

Let's take a look at what might have been exposed in you.

**Priorities.**

At the beginning of chapter three, Michelle wrote the following in her letter:

*I made you my everything, which was wrong, and when you cheated on me with a prostitute in 1991, it devastated me.*

When God isn't the first source of our life, love, and peace and the thing that was first is taken away or blows up in our face, the foundation we were standing on collapses.

Your husband, children, parents, or friends were never supposed to be given first place in your heart.

*A lawyer asked Jesus a question, testing Him, "Teacher, which is the great commandment in the Law?" And He said to him, " 'YOU SHALL LOVE THE LORD YOUR GOD WITH ALL YOUR HEART, AND WITH ALL YOUR SOUL, AND WITH ALL YOUR MIND.' This is the great and foremost commandment. The second is like it, 'YOU SHALL LOVE YOUR NEIGHBOR AS YOURSELF.' On these two*

*commandments depend the whole Law and the
Prophets. "* —Matthew 22:35–40

This doesn't mean God caused or wanted your
husband to sin against you (and Him) so He could get at
you. Some Christians get looney with stuff like that and
pronounce judgment on God's people because of their
suffering. It's a twisted lie the enemy uses to beat people
up.

Remember, your husband made his free-will choice
to turn to sexual sin. God is quite capable of speaking to
you about His desire to be your first love without the
"help" (sin) of others.

If the Lord hasn't had first place in your heart, all
that's needed is for you to go to Him, confess, and make
some adjustments. Examine your schedule and what your
relationship with the Lord looks like. If you're distant,
draw near. If you rarely spend time with Him, create a
standing appointment in your schedule to make it happen.
Don't fall into discouragement or condemnation.

We have declared the truth that you are God's
beloved daughter. I have three daughters; when they
confess they've done something wrong to me, it's
instantly forgotten. All I want is a restored relationship;
what they did is nothing in comparison to my love for
them.

Your next priority, second only to God, should be
your husband. There is no other person in Scripture a
woman is commanded to give herself to as completely as
her husband.

He comes before your kids, parents, friends,

ministry, or hobbies. If your parents or friends want you to do something, but your husband doesn't, he comes first.

*For this reason a man shall leave his father and his mother, and be joined to his wife; and they shall become one flesh.*
—Genesis 2:24

If you haven't "left" your father and mother emotionally so you can give yourself completely to your husband, cut the cord. If your parents or extended family are toxic to your marriage, you may need to set firm boundaries or put distance between you. This doesn't mean you can't honor your relationship with your parents, but that your husband comes first and you won't allow anyone to interfere with your God-given priorities.

Having four kids I know that mothers can get overwhelmed; however, there is always a way to honor your spouse and keep the marriage a priority if you're willing to look for one. Hire a babysitter so you can go on a date; some churches offer babysitting as a ministry. Ask friends or non-toxic relatives to have your kids over for an overnight stay so you can get away with your husband. Pray for a creative solution.

**Fear.**

On March 11, 1997, our second son Scott was born. There were problems from the moment he arrived. Scott was having a seizure and couldn't breathe on his own.

They put him on a ventilator; he started breathing. After running tests, they discovered that his cerebellum wasn't properly formed; he wouldn't be able to live a normal life.

Four days later, the doctors made the decision to take him off the ventilator to see if he could breathe without it.

The next day, Scott stopped breathing. As Michelle and I held our son and watched him pass from this life to the next, I blurted out, "God, please show us something."

Instantly, Scott smiled. I couldn't believe it; he was basically brain dead and yet, there was a strong sense of God's presence in the room, then Scott was gone.

Losing a child had been one of my greatest fears. The grief and sorrow were overwhelming. It was a year before I was able to make it through the day without feeling like I wanted to cry.

The Lord may take us to a place where our deepest fears lie. Many wives fear losing their husband and being left alone, perhaps as a single mom.

*Passing through the valley of Baca (weeping) they make it a spring; The early rain also covers it with blessings.*
—Psalm 84:6

It is in the valley of sorrow where we can know and experience the Lord more intimately and powerfully than before. In spite of the pain, God is more than enough. This is the place where fear is conquered and love reigns. When you know beyond a shadow of a doubt that the Lord loves you passionately and you've experienced His love, no matter what happens, even if your heart is broken, your faith will carry you through.

This is one of the silver linings in your journey. What you're going through isn't an out-of-control freak situation where you will be overwhelmed in darkness and without hope for the rest of your life. You, as a beloved daughter of Christ, will never be alone. Sometimes the cracks in our faith need to be exposed so the foundation can be rebuilt.

**Your heart.**
The heart is the key to the Christian life.

*Watch over your heart with all diligence,*
*For from it flow the springs of life.*
—Proverbs 4:23

Many Christians are living under the illusion that Bible knowledge and theology are enough for their walk with God. Or they base their sense of self-worth on doing things for God such as ministry or taking care of their family.

From 2007 to 2009, I went through an intense period of testing. The two stories about spiritual warfare in chapter nine from 2009 were a part of it. God used that time to reveal deep places in my heart I hadn't been aware of.

Fear was there; so were doubt, anger, and rebellion. He also opened my eyes to something that horrified me— it was far worse than any sexual sin I'd committed.

Pride. There was a mountain of it. It was so ugly and hideous it made me sick. I hated everything it represented. Before 2007, I'd used ministry as a vehicle to build myself up. When my pride was exposed, I didn't want anything to do with ministry, and walked away from Blazing Grace. I thought I was done with it.

The Lord had a different plan. He used that suffering to split my mountain of pride down the middle. He taught me about overcoming fear, humility, trust, and especially, obedience. He exposed my distorted motives when it came to ministry and revealed that my priorities were wrong. I was first, ministry second; God and my wife followed. He used the fires of that red-hot furnace to burn away sin in my heart and purify me.

After four years away from ministry, God orchestrated the events that brought me back. The nonprofit organization I had given Blazing Grace to lost funding, and gave it back to me. By 2012, I was in the flow again, but this time, with a different heart.

I refer to the suffering of those years as my anchor of humility. This doesn't mean I don't get tempted with pride or that it's not still lurking in my flesh, but that the mountain was reduced to rubble and I'm far more sensitive to it than before. If I'm tempted to think more highly of myself than I should, I need only remember the broken mess I was in 2007 and 2008, and I'm anchored to humility once more.

Today I see ministry as a privilege. It is not a right, nor does God need me involved.

My wife comes before ministry; if an opportunity arises, I ask her if she's okay with it. If she's not, I don't

131

go. Prior to 2007 I did what I wanted.

## Your core beliefs.

*For as he thinks within himself, so he is.*
—Proverbs 23:7

Our core belief system sets the course of our lives. If we believe God is distant, uncaring, or cruel, our relationship with Him will flounder and we will be prone to bouts of depression, discouragement, or anger.

If we believe God is faithful and His love for us is secure, no matter how difficult the trial, we will still suffer, yet our relationship with Him will keep us steadied.

Knowing the truth isn't the same as believing it. Most, if not all, of the men in bondage to sexual sin I've worked with know Scripture. Some are pastors. The truth hadn't made it to their heart because it was blocked with sin, shame, lies, and pride.

If we believe something that doesn't line up with Scripture, such as, "God is pleased with me because I'm in ministry and take care of my family; nothing bad will happen to me," our trials will blow that out of the water. Suffering is guaranteed in this life for Christ-followers (II Timothy 3:12).

As you walk this road, the Lord may open your eyes to lies you might have bought in to about yourself, God, your spouse, or life. Suffering has a way of bringing clarity and sifting out the distorted beliefs that have kept us in bondage or crippled our relationships with God and others.

I encourage you to get alone with the Lord and ask Him to open your eyes to what the trial of your husband's sexual sin has exposed in your heart. Perhaps you already had a sense, or maybe He used this chapter to open your eyes.

If there's sin, the remedy is to confess it, leave it at the cross, and receive God's cleansing (I John 1:9). Don't beat yourself up.

If the Lord is performing surgery on your heart it's because He loves you. It's more proof you're His daughter. When He brings conviction it's always to heal and restore.

God is a gentle doctor. While suffering is hard, the end result is always worth it, if we cooperate with His healing process.

# NOTES

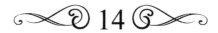

## 14

## Lies, the Truth, and Healing

*So Jesus was saying to those Jews who had believed Him,*
*"If you continue in My word, then you are truly disciples*
*of Mine; and you will know the truth, and the truth will*
*make you free."*
—John 8:31–32

A young daughter loves and adores her dad. But, he's distracted with work and his hobbies. Emotionally, he's withdrawn and non-affectionate; she rarely hears "I love you." She grows up questioning her self-worth and whether she can be loved.

She marries a guy, who, unknown to her, has an addiction to pornography. The beginning of their marriage is okay, but over time, because of porn's isolating effects, her husband becomes withdrawn and distracted. Affection dries up, and she rarely hears "I love you."

Just like Dad.

When a woman marries a man who parallels her father and there is an unresolved wound from childhood, the pain from her husband's sexual sin will cut into her first wound. She will face twice the amount of anger and pain. This is why some women transform into raging volcanoes with hair-trigger volatility, ready to blow at the slightest touch. Others fall into a hole of depression so deep and dark that they collapse into a heap of hopelessness.

A wife with unresolved childhood wounds cannot fully heal; neither can her marriage. Her attempts to deal with triggers, contain her anger, and overcome fear fail often, not for lack of trying or because God isn't there, but because her pain and emotions are driving her with such force that she's overwhelmed.

Women with unresolved trauma, such as physical or sexual abuse, have it harder. Ongoing verbal torment by the father or mother where the child's self-esteem was shredded can be just as painful.

If you have deep, unresolved abuse or trauma, this may be a dangerous time for you. Rage can harden your heart to the point where you walk away from the Lord. Some women have gone so far that they committed a crime; I know of one wife who shot her husband.

Women who feel trapped in a deep hole of depression may become suicidal. It's important you realize there's a lot at stake and the consequences for not resolving your core issues could be severe. Your personality, background, how your family of origin dealt with conflict, and the depth of your wounds are determining factors.

Even if your family treated you well growing up, all it takes is for one lie to take hold at an early age to cause wreckage and pain well into adulthood. A woman who was neglected or verbally abused by Dad may internalize lies such as, "I can't be loved as I am"; "I must earn love"; or "the only way I can be loved is if I give my body up for sex." She may spend years searching for love and acceptance in ways that never satisfy. Her emptiness rubs her core wound raw and proves it's the truth (so she thinks). She may isolate herself from God and others by withdrawing into a protective shell.

For some of these wounded women, sex and emotional intimacy are terrifying experiences that put their heart at risk. Others may use intimacy or their husband as a Band-Aid to cover up their pain.

If any of the above is you, we have work to do. I suggest you get a journal so you can write out your feelings. Also, it's important that you are able to share what follows with a safe friend who can pray for you.

The first step is to come to terms with what happened. Many adult children try to protect their parents with statements like, "Mom and Dad did the best they could . . . I know they loved me, they just didn't show it . . . they came from a messed-up family so it wasn't all their fault."

People prove their love by their actions and their words. If your husband never told you that he loved you before you got married, or if he never hugged you, would you have believed he loved you? Would you have married him? Probably not.

It's the same with Mom and Dad. If they didn't express love to you growing up, the two people with the most profound influence in your life communicated a message that you were of little value.

One woman I worked with told me her father never told her he loved her for the first twelve years of her life; neither did he hug her. One day, out of frustration, she asked him, "Do you love me?" His immediate response was, "No! Not when you act like you are now!"

Not only was this woman unloved by Dad, but now he communicated the message to her that she had to earn his love by "being good." Since she didn't experience his love growing up, the next lie she internalized was that finding love was next to impossible.

It's painful to come to terms with the idea that we were unloved as a child by our parents. We want to believe they loved us passionately because the perception of our self-worth was intertwined with how they treated us.

Just as those who have cancer need to face their disease so they can begin treatment, so the only way you can move toward healing is to accept what happened in childhood.

Afterward, pour your heart out into your journal and share with your safe friend or counselor. What did you want from your father or mother that you didn't get? How did what happened affect you then, and how is it affecting you now? What was lost?

Allow yourself to grieve what could have been. There's no opportunity for a do-over. What they did or said can't be taken back. If your parent(s) passed away and you weren't able to reconcile with them, the grieving process may have more significance because the relationship can't be mended. Maybe it couldn't when they were alive.

After you've worked through the grieving process, it's time to look at how you interpreted what happened and the messages you internalized, which formed your core beliefs.

Let's take a girl who was sexually molested by a man as an example. Those who were sexually abused may have great difficulty trusting others. They may feel ashamed, dirty, and soiled.

Since sexual abuse is a severe violation of boundaries, they may be plagued with bouts of rage. Pushing people away is common to avoid pain. They may struggle with depression and hopelessness.

A person who's sexually abused may internalize the following lies:

"Because I'm dirty, no one will love me as I am."

"I dare not trust anyone with my heart. If I do, I will be violated or hurt again."

"What happened was my fault."

"I hate men and what they do to women."

"I cannot be loved by a man unless I allow them to use me by giving them sex."

A woman who rarely if ever heard "I love you" or was hugged from Dad growing up might buy in to these lies:

"I must do something to earn love."

"Since I've never received love, I must not be worthy of it."

"In order to receive love, I must (fill in the blank: "Give myself up for sex, allow others to manipulate or use me, turn to food or drugs for comfort, be a good girl by working hard at doing what good Christian women are supposed to do at home and in ministry").

"A man can't love me as I am."

"God doesn't love me as I am."

These lies are poison to your heart.

They must be exposed, removed, and replaced with the truth. Otherwise, your heart will continue to be corrupted with anger, pain, and hopelessness, blocking you and your marriage from healing and restoration.

Get alone with God and ask Him to reveal every lie you've bought in to. You can use the lists above to get you started. Write them in your journal.

Now ask the Lord to lead you to the truths that will replace every lie. For example, "God doesn't love me as I am," would be swapped for, "I am His beloved daughter." Then, "I must do something to earn God's love" would be replaced with, "It's impossible for me to do anything to earn God's love. That's okay, because all of my sins were paid for at the cross, and I am His beloved daughter." "I dare not trust anyone," could be replaced with, "I can trust the Lord with all of my heart because He loves me and always has my best interests in mind.

As for trusting people, although I was hurt by others in the past, I have several safe friends I can trust who will not violate me. Not everyone is like my abuser. I will use the wisdom God gives me to know how much trust I should extend in every situation. I need not give everyone all of my heart. God will give me the wisdom I need whenever I ask Him (James 1:5)."

In the bonus section at the back of this book, there is

a chapter with lies and the verses you can use to replace them that might help you.

After you've recorded your new set of core beliefs in your journal, you can do the next steps with the Lord, and with your friend or support group, which are to:

Confess each lie you've bought in to as sin, and renounce its grip on your life.

Ask the Lord to cement the truths that are your new core beliefs in your heart.

Ask for the filling of the Holy Spirit and the wisdom and strength to walk in the truth from this day forward.

Ask for prayer from your friend or group for the above, and for healing.

After you've spent years allowing these lies to have their way with you, it may take time to get used to living in the truth. Your emotions may scream, "This can't be true!" while the Holy Spirit is whispering, "Yes, it is; I love you." You can go to God and say, "Lord, you say it's true, and you never lie, so I'm going to receive the gifts of your love in spite of how I feel or what's going on with my husband. Thank you for helping me and walking with me."

Thanking God for the truth is a way of receiving His grace.

If a banker approached you and said, "You won the lottery. I'm going to give you a hundred million dollars," you wouldn't say, "No, I'm not worthy. Give it to someone else." After you verified he wasn't tricking you, your response should be to extend your hands, receive the gift, and say, "Thank you!"

*Blessed be the God and Father of our Lord Jesus Christ,*
*who has blessed us with every spiritual blessing in the*
*heavenly places in Christ, just as He chose us in Him*
*before the foundation of the world, that we would be holy*
*and blameless before Him.*
*In love, He predestined us to adoption as sons through*
*Jesus Christ to Himself, according to the kind intention*
*of His will, to the praise of the glory of His grace, which*
*He freely bestowed on us in the Beloved.*
*In Him we have redemption through His blood, the*
*forgiveness of our trespasses, according to the riches of*
*His grace which He lavished on us.*
—Ephesians 1:3–8

You're already a spiritual billionaire; God has lavished you with His love and every spiritual blessing from heaven. If you've been poisoned with lies, it's been as if God has been showering you with love for years but you've been holding a black umbrella over your heart. Remove the umbrella of lies, and you'll get drenched with the downpour of His grace.

Many Christians have no idea of how much they've been given. They're distracted or choked, or they're ensnared in sin or lies. Take off the blinders, and "Wow!" you'll understand that God has done immeasurably more than you've imagined or understood.

After you've received your new set of core beliefs and the love of God that accompanies them, it's time for forgiveness. To lift those last pieces of bitterness from your heart requires that you grant the person who hurt you a full pardon. When you forgive, you're giving up your right to hold anything against them and transferring the burden of their sin to the Lord. Forgiveness seals your heart from bitterness and fills it with grace and peace.

If you get stuck and are having a hard time forgiving, it's okay. If the wound is deep, you may need God's help. Go to Him, confess you're stuck, and ask for the grace and Holy Spirit-infused power to forgive. The enemy may come back at you and remind you of what others did to hurt you, or he may try to get you to bite on the old lies. You have all you need to overcome every attack. Step back, and examine what's happening.

If an old lie such as, "God doesn't love me as I am," tries to intrude in your mind, you can respond with, "No, I'm not buying it. I am God's beloved daughter and He died for my sins at the cross." If the enemy keeps coming, command him to leave your presence as I described in the chapter on warfare.

If your parents are still alive, use wisdom. If you've reconciled, that's great, but you're not obligated to share everything with them.

Don't feel like you need to tell them how they've hurt you or that you've forgiven them. If their heart is hard or they wouldn't be able to receive what you might share, let it go. You could do more damage than good.

Remember to use wisdom in all of your relationships. Talking to your safe friend or support group and asking for prayer is always a good idea. Sometimes the best thing you can do is to set healthy boundaries with others.

Telling everyone everything and expecting them to respond how you want them to is a recipe for disaster. If your parents or friends aren't safe people, guard your heart.

Some wounds take longer to heal and involve more prayer, sharing with your friends, and additional touches from the Lord. God didn't heal everyone in the Bible in the same way or timing. It's okay if the process takes longer; keep pressing on.

# NOTES

## 15

## The If, When, and Why of Forgiving Your Husband

"How many times *should I forgive my husband for acting out with porn?"*

Then Peter came and said to Him, "Lord, how often shall my brother sin against me and I forgive him? Up to seven times?" Jesus said to him, "I do not say to you, up to seven times, but up to seventy times seven.

*"For this reason the kingdom of heaven may be compared to a king who wished to settle accounts with his slaves. When he had begun to settle them, one who owed him ten thousand talents was brought to him. But since he did not have the means to repay, his lord commanded him to be sold, along with his wife and children and all that he had, and repayment to be made. So the slave fell to the ground and prostrated himself before him, saying, 'Have patience with me and I will repay you everything.' And the lord of that slave felt compassion and released him and forgave him the debt.*

146

*But that slave went out and found one of his fellow slaves
who owed him a hundred denarii; and he seized him and
began to choke him, saying, 'Pay back what you owe.'
So his fellow slave fell to the ground and began to plead
with him, saying, 'Have patience with me and I will
repay you.'
But he was unwilling and went and threw him in prison
until he should pay back what was owed.
So when his fellow slaves saw what had happened, they
were deeply grieved and came and reported to their lord
all that had happened.
Then summoning him, his lord \*said to him, 'You wicked
slave, I forgave you all that debt because you pleaded
with me. Should you not also have had mercy on your
fellow slave, in the same way that I had mercy on you?'
And his lord, moved with anger, handed him over to the
torturers until he should repay all that was owed him.
My heavenly Father will also do the same to you, if each
of you does not forgive his brother from your heart."*
—Matthew 18:21–35

God's answer to the If is: every time, no matter what
your husband does. As Matthew 18 shows, the penalty
for not forgiving is severe. Before you draw your final
conclusion, we'll address what forgiveness is not in the
context of a marriage that has been torn by adultery or
porn in a moment.

The next question is when. How long you should
wait before forgiving your husband?

Jesus forgave His tormentors while He was suffering

on the cross in front of the men who put Him there. His answer to "when" could be "as soon as you're able."

For many wives, forgiving their husband immediately after the initial disclosure is unreasonable. It can take weeks or longer just to recover from the initial shock and adjust to the reality of their husband's sin. Forgiveness from the heart is a rough one to expect if you're still in shock.

I've heard of one wife who, after the truth came out, forgave him several days later. Other women take months, some years. Everyone's background and circumstances are different. Setting a timeline for when a wife should forgive her husband is unrealistic, if not borderline abusive.

One wife who had held on to her anger for several years said she'd earned the right to be angry. Indeed she had.., the question is whether making friends with resentment is in her best interest.

Long-term anger increases your risk of heart attack and stroke, weakens your immune system, can trigger anxiety and depression, and shortens your life span. Anger isn't something you want hanging around for long. [1]

---

[1] Debbie Strong, Everyday Health, "7 Ways Is Ruining Your Health." Accessed January 5, 2017.

http://www.everydayhealth.com/news/ways-anger-ruining-your-health/.

At the age of fourteen, I was sexually molested by a trusted female adult family member. My mind couldn't wrap itself around the reality of what happened, and the memory was buried in the recesses of my mind.

Eight years later, I started seeing a female counselor. She started poking and prodding, until one day she said, "You have a hatred for women, don't you?" I was stunned and couldn't see how it could be possible. I hadn't told her I had a lust problem with women; I thought I worshiped them.

She kept at it and started asking about my relationships with women growing up, until one day the memory of being molested forced its way into my consciousness.

I was furious, and started bouncing between rage and depression like a yo-yo. The counselor had me process my feelings for several months, until I stopped seeing her when we moved to Colorado.

For the next twenty years, I continued to struggle with anger and depression. Finally, another counselor asked the question that started me on the path to healing: "Have you ever forgiven the person who molested you?"

"Uhhhh, I guess I haven't."

At his advice, I wrote the person who molested me a one-page letter. I briefly described what they did and how it affected me, and finished by telling them I forgave them.

As soon as I mailed the letter, there was an instant sense that a heavy weight had been lifted from my heart. The anger and resentment were gone. I finally had peace.

When I wrote the letter, I was nervous about how the

other person would respond; now it didn't matter. The peace and freedom I possessed outweighed anything they might say.

I received her response two weeks later. She wrote: "Did that make you feel better?" That was it. No acknowledgment of what happened, no apology.

I thought it was weird, almost surreal (how can someone check out after they're told they sexually molested you?), but it didn't matter. I wasn't going back to a life of bitterness. Twenty years was enough.

You can hang on to your anger as long as you like; God gave you the free will to do so. The only way you will find healing and peace is to forgive your husband.

It's possible your husband may not respond well if you tell him you forgive him; receiving forgiveness requires that the offending party takes ownership of their sin. He may check out or deflect responsibility like the woman who molested me. How he responds is of secondary importance; focus on your first priority, which is to choose between peace and healing through forgiveness, or anger and bitterness.

If Jesus made a contrite response a condition for forgiveness, He couldn't have offered it on the cross. None of His accusers apologized after He asked the Father to forgive them. If I made an apology a condition for forgiving the woman who molested me, my heart would be rock-hard. I would be an ugly person to be around.

Forgiving your husband does not mean:

You're a doormat. It takes strength of character and humility to forgive another person, especially if they've hurt you.

You're obligated to trust him. Trust and forgiveness are two separate issues.

While you must forgive because God commands it (and for your own sanity), your husband must earn every ounce of trust back.

Your husband will change. If he's still lost in the fog of self-absorption, it could take time before he understands the value of your forgiveness.

You won't have to forgive him again. If he keeps sinning sexually you will need to forgive him again.

He gets off the hook with the boundaries and consequences you've set. You are God's beloved daughter, and shouldn't accept anything less than total commitment and the action steps he must take to restore your marriage.

Fifteen years after I confessed my adultery to Michelle in 1991, I realized I'd never heard her say she'd forgiven me. Although our relationship had been restored long ago, I didn't want to assume I knew where her heart was, so I asked her if she'd forgiven me.

She wrote me a letter, and read it one night. I'll never forget it. She described how I'd hurt her, then told me she forgave me.

We were both in tears; it was one of the most tender moments of my life. Her forgiveness was a precious gift I could never earn or repay.

There are many husbands who will be overwhelmed in awe that their wives would forgive them for their sexual sin. Hopefully, your husband will be one of them.

Keep short accounts with anger; express it, forgive,

and move on. If your husband keeps sinning sexually, continue to stand firm and hold the line of your boundaries and consequences.

Peace and healing are infinitely better than bitterness and depression.

The choice is yours.

# NOTES

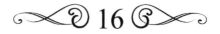

## 16

## A Story of Healing

This allegory provides a picture of what healing looks like for you and your husband.

In his early years, the Little Boy was a happy kid, with a fun, adventurous spirit. He loved playing with his army toys and pretending to be the hero who saves the day. He would imagine himself as Rambo—fearless, determined, and with big biceps, able to jump into battle at a moment's notice against overwhelming odds and win. Or he'd picture himself as Braveheart, a leader whose courage and integrity was admired by both men and women. Yes sir, that's the kind of man the Little Boy wanted to be. He would paint his face blue and dash around the backyard, slashing at bushes and trees with his toy sword, taking on imaginary foes in desperate battle.

Most of all, the Little Boy wanted to be like his daddy; he was everything the Little Boy wanted to be: smart, strong, and tough. He was proud of his daddy, and would boast to other little boys that his daddy could whip theirs. He loved it when they would wrestle and laugh together or talk about men stuff . . . when his daddy was home, that is. His daddy traveled a lot for his job, and was gone often. It made the Little Boy sad that he couldn't have more time with him.

But the Little Boy notices that other little boys don't get sad; they're too rough 'n' rowdy to feel things like that, so he decides to be a rough 'n' rowdy boy too. Although they say and do things his parents have told him not to, which gets him into trouble, it makes him feel good when the other boys tell him how cool he is.

One day, his mommy and daddy have to go somewhere, and they leave him and his little sister with Uncle Frank to stay the night at his house. The Little Boy had always thought Uncle Frank was weird; his uncle is quiet, and every once in a while he would see Uncle Frank looking at him in a strange way that made him feel uncomfortable.

That night, Uncle Frank seems happy. They watch fun movies together and have popcorn, and he lets them stay up for a while. When it gets late, Uncle Frank puts his little sister to bed first, in a guest bedroom in the house. Then Uncle Frank brings the Little Boy into his bedroom . . . and does some horrible things to him . . . that involve touching the Little Boy's private parts.

Afterward, the Little Boy is so sick that he throws up. He wants to run away but is too afraid. "If you tell anyone what happened," Uncle Frank tells him, "I'll do this to you again." The Little Boy promises he won't say a word.

Over the next few years, the Little Boy starts to change. Some days he gets angry for no reason; on others, he wants to cry a lot. He wants to tell his daddy what happened so he can pound Uncle Frank, but his daddy is gone even more now. His mommy and daddy are fighting a lot too. He's now afraid of being touched by other people. He hates family get-togethers, because Aunt Susie, who has to hug and kiss everyone, is always there. Some nights, he has nightmares about what happened with Uncle Frank; when this happens he often wakes up shivering in fear.

One day a few years later, the Little Boy is at Jimmie's house. Jimmie is another rough 'n' rowdy boy, and he and the Little Boy hang out together a lot. Jimmie goes to a hiding place in his room and shows the Little Boy his collection of magazines he has—magazines with lots of shocking pictures of little girls. Although the Little Boy instinctively knows these magazines are bad, the pictures excite him. "Go on, take one home," laughs Jimmie. "I have plenty more."

The Little Boy takes the magazine home and looks at it a lot. He remembers what Uncle Frank did to him, and how it felt, and does it to himself. *This is fun*, the Little Boy thinks. Soon, he has his own hidden collection of magazines, just like Jimmie.

One day, the Little Boy's mommy and daddy start going to church. They'd recently heard about someone named Jesus, and going to church seemed to be what people did who wanted to know more about Him. In church, the Little Boy learns that Jesus is God and that He loves him and died on the cross for him. He hears that bad people go to hell, and that Christians, people who love Jesus, go to heaven. The Little Boy doesn't want to go to hell, so he decides to become a Christian. Immediately, something strange happens inside. The Little Boy finds he doesn't want to be rough 'n' rowdy anymore—he wants to please Jesus.

The Little Boy goes to several churches over the years with his parents and notices the pastors say different things about God. One pastor screams, "If you sin a lot, you will go to hell!" which scares the little boy, so he starts trying his best to be good. Another says, "You need to learn everything in this book and do it so you can please God." Another pastor says, "God loves you." The Little Boy likes to hear this, but doesn't always feel like God loves him, especially after he looks at his magazines. *Besides, if God loves me, why did He let Uncle Frank do those things to me?* he wonders.

One day at church, the Little Boy meets a pretty Little Girl in a blue dress. This Little Girl is special. She knocks him out like no other little girl has before. He loves everything about her—how she looks, talks, and thinks. When they're together, he's happy and doesn't want to leave her. Soon, they become best friends.

Growing up, the Little Girl loved to dance. A few years back, when her school was putting on a play, she was going to be the main character. This play meant everything to her. She spent several months practicing for it, and would often spend two hours a day practicing her moves. She wanted everything to be perfect.

The day before the play, her mommy took her to a store to buy a beautiful, frilly white dress and new shoes, just for the play. *I can't wait for my daddy to see me in this dress,* she thought, as she looked at her image in the mirror at the store. He would be so proud. When they arrived home, they saw there was a note on the kitchen counter. Her mommy started crying after she read it. "He left us," she said. The Little Girl's daddy had left them for another mommy, who had two other little girls. Brokenhearted, the Little Girl never wore that dress again, neither did she participate in the play. She told the school she was too sick to dance, and another little girl took her part.

It wasn't long before the Little Girl and the Little Boy decided to become best friends for life. Both of them are excited; now they'll be loved by someone who won't hurt them. In the excitement of getting married, the Little Boy throws his collection of magazines in the trash; he won't need them now that he has his Little Girl.

For the first few months, their marriage is a lot of fun; they laugh, kiss, and hug each other a lot. Being best friends for life is great. But then, something starts going wrong. The Little Boy starts feeling like he did before they were best friends for life—angry, scared, and like he wants to cry a lot. He stops talking to his Little Girl as much, and they stop kissing. The Little Girl feels hurt and unloved, and starts pushing her Little Boy to talk to tell her what's wrong. Problem is, the more she pushes him, the more scared he gets, and they end up fighting a lot.

One day, while the Little Girl is away at the store, the Little Boy discovers he can look at pictures like those in the magazines he used to have by using his computer to get on the Internet. He remembers how good this used to make him feel. *This is the only safe way I can be loved*, he tells himself. He starts looking at the pictures of other little girls on the computer and touching himself often, sneaking out to their computer room after his Little Girl had gone to sleep, or when she is out running errands.

Late one night, the Little Girl wakes up after the Little Boy has left their room to get on the computer. Puzzled by his absence, she walks into their computer room, and is horrified to see her Little Boy touching himself as he is looking at pictures of other little girls on their computer. She can't believe what her best friend for life is doing, and starts crying.

The Little Boy is embarrassed and feels awful. How could he have hurt his Little Girl this way? "I'll never do it again. I'm sorry," he promises her. The Little Girl wants to trust her Little Boy more than anything; although she's deeply hurt, she believes him.

In the weeks that follow, the pictures from those images keep coming back to the Little Boy's mind, and he eventually breaks his promise to the Little Girl. *It'll be okay as long as she doesn't find out,* he thinks. *What she doesn't know won't hurt her.* She asks him from time to time if he's still looking at the pictures, but he always lies, not wanting to hurt her again.

Even though her Little Boy says he isn't looking at the pictures anymore, there's something about the way he acts that doesn't feel right to the Little Girl. He doesn't laugh much anymore, and he's quiet a lot; he rarely kisses her. When she asks him if everything's okay, he gets angry and defensive, as if he's irritated that she could even ask him this question. Even though he says nothing's wrong, their friendship seems to be dying.

One day a few months later, as the Little Girl is typing a letter on their computer at home, she hits a key by mistake—and is horrified when a shocking picture of another little girl pops up to the screen. Hoping this is an isolated incident, she calls one of her friends, who tells her how to find where pictures are stored on the computer, and is stunned to find hundreds more of them. From the dates on the files, it looks like her Little Boy has been looking at pictures of other little girls every day. *How could I have believed him all this time?* she asks herself through tears of anger and hurt.

This is too much for her to take; she quickly writes a note that says, "You've hurt me too much, and I can't trust you. I'm sorry, but I can't be your best friend for life anymore," packs her bags, and leaves their home.

Later that evening, the Little Boy is puzzled to come home to a dark house. "Usually she leaves a light on— what's going . . ." and then he sees her note. "Oh no! What have I done?" he screams. His first instinct is to rush to the computer and look at more of those pictures to forget about his loneliness, but then, he realizes, "This junk is the reason why I lost my Little Girl. I don't want it anymore I want her." In a panic, he calls his Little Girl at her Mommy's house and promises to be good, but she refuses to listen. "You've lied too many times. I can't trust you again with my heart," she says, and hangs up.

That night, the Little Boy cries more than any other time in his life. He thinks about God and all the things he's heard said at church. He knows what the Bible says but has disobeyed it for years. *Maybe I've sinned so much I'm going to hell* he wonders. *Maybe Jesus doesn't love me anymore.*

"God, I've made a mess of my life and I don't know what to do. If you're there, please help me," he prays. The Little Boy is so sick from sadness that he feels like he wants to throw up. Finally, late at night, he falls asleep.

As the Little Boy is sleeping, Jesus appears to him in a dream. He and Jesus are standing outside of a house that looks strangely familiar.

Jesus is wearing a bright white robe; light emanates from Him. There is a look of compassion in Jesus's eyes as He asks the Little Boy, "Will you let me heal you?"

Although the Little Boy is scared, the look on Jesus's face puts him at ease.

"I think so. What do I have to do?"

"Enter this house with Me."

Suddenly, the Little Boy remembers whose house they're standing in front of: it's Uncle Frank's.

"I can't go in there. I can't," the Little Boy says in a terrified whisper.

"The choice is yours. You can stay where you are, if you like, but this will be as good as your life will get."

The Little Boy thinks back to where his actions had taken him, and how he'd lost his Little Girl.

"Okay."

In an instant, the Little Boy and Jesus are standing in Uncle Frank's bedroom—the place where those horrible things were done to the Little Boy. He feels sick to his stomach and angry. He hates Uncle Frank.

"Why?" he asks. "Jesus, why did you let this happen

161

to me??"

Jesus looks at him with a steady gaze: "Will knowing why make a difference?" He asks softy.

"I . . ." and then, the Little Boy realizes that Jesus is right. Knowing *why* can't change what happened. A sense of utter hopelessness washes over him, and the Little Boy starts crying.

Jesus extends his right hand out to him and says:

"I love you, My child."

Upon hearing this, the Little Boy rushes into Jesus's arms and lets it all out—years of pain, shame, and sorrow are poured out with deep, heaving sobs. As he allows Jesus to comfort him, the warmth of God's love breaks into his heart, healing the Little Boy's heart. God does love him, just as the Bible says.

"My child, you've been in this room all of your life, and it's kept you trapped in pain and sin. Are you ready to leave it?"

"Yes Lord!"

"To leave this room, you must forgive your uncle."

The Little Boy hesitated for a moment; this was unexpected. Uncle Frank doesn't deserve forgiveness—heck, he'd never even asked for it. And yet, the joy in the Little Boy's heart is too good to mess up with bitterness any longer; what further use would his anger serve?

"I forgive Uncle Frank," the Little Boy says firmly.

Jesus smiles: "You must never return to that room again."

Instantly, the Little Boy finds that He and Jesus are back in the living room of his home. The only light in the house comes from Jesus—all the lights in the house are still off.

"Can I have my Little Girl back now?" the Little Boy asks.

"It's up to her. If she won't allow me to heal her as you've done, she may not come back. There are many little girls who've been hurt by their little boys who don't return. No matter what happens, I must be your first best friend now, not the Little Girl. If she should return to you again, you must resolve to let her into your heart on a consistent basis to keep your relationship alive. She wants you, not the breadcrumbs of your life. Will you trust Me, no matter what happens?"

After hours of crying at her mommy's house, the Little Girl has made up her mind: she's not going back to her Little Boy. *Maybe the Little Boy I first met never existed,* she wonders. She feels hard, cold, and empty inside. *I won't let anyone hurt me like that again,* she promises herself.

That night, Jesus appears to her in a dream. He and the Little Girl are standing outside the house where she grew up.

"Will you let me heal you?" He asks.

"Heal me from what?!"

Jesus is silent. He merely looks at her with an intense, yet compassionate gaze that melts her heart like a wax candle.

"Okay," she says.

Suddenly, they are in the kitchen, standing in front of the counter, and there's a note on it—the one her daddy wrote when he left.

"Where have you been all of my life?" the Little Girl

asks. "Why did my father leave us? And why did you give me a Little Boy who looks at pictures of other little girls??"

Softly, Jesus repeats his original question: "Will you let me heal you?"

*Why isn't He answering my questions?* she wonders as she nods again.

There's a long rectangular box sitting on the kitchen counter. Jesus walks up to it, takes it, and then hands it to the Little Girl. In the box is the dress her mother had bought her for the dance.

"Will you dance for Me?" Jesus asks.

The Little Girl can't believe what she just heard; the King of the Universe is inviting her to dance for Him.

"Okay," she whispers, trying to hold back tears.

Suddenly, they are in a school auditorium. The Little Girl is wearing the white dress and shoes that her mommy bought her, and is standing center stage; all lights are on her. There are many people in the crowd, but it's dark and she can't make out their faces, except for one. There, seated in the center of the front row, is Jesus, who's beaming at her like a proud father.

Music starts playing, and the Little Girl begins to dance, like she's never danced before; her timing is perfect. As she dances, she can't take her eyes off of Jesus, who is watching her every move with interest.

A few minutes later, the Little Girl finishes her dance, and there is thunderous applause; the lights come on, and she sees that the auditorium is packed with angels. As she stands there, stunned, Jesus stands up, walks up to her, and embraces her. The Little Girl collapses to the floor, sobbing, pouring out the pain of her life out to Him. After every tear is cried out, warmth spreads through her heart, and there is joy where anger and sorrow had been. For the first time in her life, she knows she is loved.

"My daughter, will you forgive your father for leaving you?"

"Yes, Lord," the Little Girl responds eagerly.

"Will you forgive the Little Boy?"

This wasn't easy. He'd hurt her like no one else had.

"Does forgiving him mean I have to go back to him?"

"No, that choice is yours. But if you choose not to release him, you will keep your heart poisoned with bitterness."

The Little Girl thought about it for a few seconds, and then quietly says, "Okay, I forgive him. But Jesus, I can't go back to the Little Boy if he's going to hurt me like that again. Will you heal Him like you healed me?"

"Every little boy has to choose to let Me heal Him. There are many who don't. If you want to know the answer to this, go and ask him. If you choose to stay, you will need to accept him as he is to make the relationship work. I have made him like he is for a purpose, and your role will be to build him up into My purpose."

Two weeks later, it's six at night, and the Little Boy is home, alone. Although he hasn't heard from the Little Girl since she left, he's determined to trust Jesus no matter what happens.

There's a knock at the door. The Little Boy opens it and is stunned at the sight before him. There, standing at the doorway, is his Little Girl, wearing a white dress. She looks like an angel. Her hair is made up in a way he's never seen before, and a thin gold necklace adorns her neck. The Little Boy backs up, until his legs hit the bottom of the couch and he falls backward onto it. He doesn't know what to say, and anything he might say feels like it couldn't be enough.

The Little Girl steps in, closes the door, and sits at the other end of the couch. Both of them look at each other without speaking for several minutes.

Finally, the Little Boy musters up the courage to speak:

"I'm sorry."

The Little Girl nods.

"I've met Jesus!" he says.

"You have?" she asks. "So have I!"

Slowly, they take each other's hand . . .

and Jesus smiles.

# NOTES

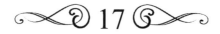

## 17

## Drawing Near

*The LORD your God is in your midst,*
*A victorious warrior.*
*He will exult over you with joy,*
*He will be quiet in His love,*
*He will rejoice over you with shouts of joy.*
—Zechariah 3:17

While your husband's recovery has a direct impact on whether your marriage is restored, the healing of your heart doesn't rely solely on him. If he spends the next several years stumbling, or doesn't recover, and you put everything on him, you'll never heal.

Conversely, your husband could break free, but you could still be left with a wounded heart.

The way to peace is through your relationship with the Lord. Everything revolves around Him—knowing what He says about you, what He wants you to do, how He sees you, and the gifts He's given you.

Learning to rely on His strength, being filled with the Holy Spirit, knowing Him, discerning His voice, and seeking Him are important pieces of your relationship

168

with Him.

I've been weaving what God says about you as His beloved daughter throughout this book because He is your primary source of healing. The Bible is not merely a book to be dissected and packaged into the church's theological box of choice, throwing out the verses we don't like and keeping the rest. God's word is an amazing, living, Holy Spirit-fired document with the power to change lives, convict, build up, and give wisdom.

When I read God's word, my primary purpose is to hear from the Lord. Before I begin, I ask Him to speak to me and help me understand what He's saying. The Holy Spirit breathes His word into my heart and grants me the grace of understanding and discernment.

There are parts of God's character and power I have a hard time getting my mind around. How can one Being know the thoughts of more than seven billion people simultaneously? How do you design a man or woman? Just engineering the human brain, with its billions of neurons, is way out of our league.

Yet, because God has repeatedly spoken to me over the years, I know He hears every one of my prayers and wants to spend time with me, just as He does with you.

In the past, most of my time with Him revolved around my lists: "Lord, please set me free from sexual sin, heal my marriage, fix my wife, resolve my problems at work, keep my kids safe, give us godly leaders, bring the lost to salvation . . ."

And then after I sinned (which was often), it was, "God please forgive me, heal me, cleanse me, set me free . . ."

See what's going on in these prayers? It's not that what I'm asking for is wrong, but they're all about me and what I want God to do for me.

My self-absorption prevented me from receiving forgiveness the moment I confessed my sin.

"If we confess our sins, He is faithful and just to forgive us our sins and cleanse us from all unrighteousness" (I John 1:9). When we sin, all we have to do is confess it, and we're forgiven and cleansed. Since I was locked on me, all I could see were my failures and depravity; I blindly threw up those futile, groveling prayers hoping I would one day be forgiven—when I already was.

Instead, I should have gone to God and said, "Lord, I hurt my wife last night by what I said and didn't treat her with kindness. Please help me to love her like you want me to. Thank you for forgiving me." No groveling, begging, or bargaining for forgiveness, or self-condemnation.

One reason people give up on prayer is because they don't understand there are times when the Lord wants them to keep pressing in.

*Now He was telling them a parable to show that at all times they ought to pray and not to lose heart, saying, "In a certain city there was a judge who did not fear God and did not respect man. There was a widow in that city, and she kept coming to*

*him, saying, 'Give me legal protection from my opponent.'*
*For a while he was unwilling; but afterward he said to himself, 'Even though I do not fear God nor respect man, yet because this widow bothers me, I will give her legal protection, otherwise by continually coming she will wear me out.'"*
*And the Lord said, "Hear what the unrighteous judge aid; now, will not God bring about justice for His elect who cry to Him day and night, and will He delay long over them? I tell you that He will bring about justice for them quickly. However, when the Son of Man comes, will He find faith on the earth?"* —Luke 18:1–8

Recently, I struggled with resentment toward a good friend of mine. I knew them a long time and the relationship was important to me, so I started asking the Lord to lift the resentment from my heart and help me to accept them.

He began by showing me how I needed to treat that person in His word ("Love . . . bears all things, believes all things, hopes all things, endures all things . . ." —I Corinthians 13).

For the next several months, I kept praying and seeking; He responded by lifting one small piece of resentment at a time from my heart.

He showed me the other person's weaknesses, exposed a lie I'd bought in to about them, and encouraged me to take the actions of love regardless of how I felt.

Finally, my relationship with that person was

restored, and my heart was soft again.

God doesn't always work that way. Sometimes His answer is to close the door to a relationship. Others, He might want me to rest and wait.

Many Christians don't really want God; they just want Him to fix their problems or give them what they want. They do ministry, go to church, or know lots of the Bible, but they've never connected with Him and experienced the incredible blessings of soaking in His presence, having their heart tanked up with His love, or hearing His voice.

Their relationship with Him is all in their head, based on knowledge or "being good."

Once you've experienced the deep peace, rest, and love that come from knowing God, it will change you. Your circumstances may stay the same (or get worse), but you'll have joy and deep peace.

*You will seek Me and find Me when you search for Me with all your heart.* —Jeremiah 29:13

In this chapter, I want to help you draw near to the Lord.

First, take your attention off yourself. Your problems too. Everything gets sidelined; your sole focus is to be on seeking God, loving Him, and hearing from Him.

Rather than describing what drawing near to God looks like, here are several assignments that will move you into His presence.

## Listening

Find a place where you can have quiet solitude for forty-five minutes. In silence, we begin to feel and experience our heart; who we really are. Silence also tunes us into the frequency of the Holy Spirit. This may feel uncomfortable at first. That's okay; today will be a good first step.

Begin by asking the Lord to speak to you. You want to do this with Him; focused on Him. Prayer is a two-way street: most Christians know how to do the talking, but few know how to listen to God and discern His voice. In silence, our focus is on sitting at the feet of Jesus and listening.

As you settle into silence, emotions may come bubbling to the surface. That's good—your heart is beginning the process of coming alive. Roll with it and ask God to help you see and understand what He wants to show you. Don't check out. I suggest writing what comes up in your journal to record what God was saying to you so you can come back to it later.

Be flexible. There are many times when I've been in silence with God and the urge to praise Him arises. The Holy Spirit may bring a verse to my mind, expose a sin I need to face and confess, or reveal a lie I'd bought in to. Occasionally, He brings someone to mind I need to pray for. There are times when I put on praise music and just listen and soak in it. And, there are instances when I know I'm communing with God even though no words are spoken (Romans 8:26–27).

You are coming into the presence of the Living God—anything can happen. He wants you to draw near to Him, faults, shame, and all. He's promised to respond to those who approach Him with His presence. ("Draw near to God and He will draw near to you" —James 4:8.)

## Worship

I'll sometimes ask believers, "What does your relationship with the Lord look like?" Most of the time their response is something like, "Well, I read my Bible and pray." They're missing the point.

Think about your relationship with your husband. If I were to ask you what your relationship with him is like, at least in the good times or before you were married, you might have said something like, "It's awesome! We relate in many areas; his strengths complement my weaknesses. I love being with him. We laugh together, cry together, and I can share anything with him. We're going away for a weekend alone soon, and I can't wait!"

Now go back and think about my question again: "What does your relationship with God look like?"

"Read your Bible and pray" focuses on what you do. You could go on a date with your husband, get in a fight, and have a terrible time. In the same way, you can read your Bible and pray but never experience the joy of God's presence. The Pharisees memorized the first five books of the Bible and prayed, but many of them ended up in hell. Many Christians read their Bible and pray because it's what good Christians are supposed to do.

What we do doesn't describe the core of our relationship with the Lord.

This assignment is meant to facilitate your connection and relationship with God through worship. One way to look at worship is the expression of your love for the Lord.

Find a place where you can be alone in silence for forty-five to sixty minutes.

Set everything aside, even the Bible, and focus on worshiping the God who loves you. Pour your heart out to Him in love and praise. You can express your love in word, singing, or even silence. If your heart feels cold, worship Him anyway. Sometimes the act of praising God has a way of coming back to us and filling our hearts with joy. As before, focus solely on Him. Alternate between praise, silence, and more praise. Watch and wait for Him.

If Christian music helps you to worship the Lord, feel free to use it—just don't get so caught up in the song that you get sidetracked from worshiping God.

### Rest

*For thus the Lord GOD, the Holy One of Israel, has said,*
*"In repentance and rest you will be saved,*
*In quietness and trust is your strength."*
*But you were not willing,*
*And you said, "No, for we will flee on horses,"*
*Therefore you shall flee!*
*"And we will ride on swift horses,"*

*Therefore those who pursue you shall be swift.*
*One thousand will flee at the threat of one man;*
*You will flee at the threat of five,*
*Until you are left as a flag on a mountain top*
*And as a signal on a hill.*
*Therefore the LORD longs to be gracious to you,*
*And therefore He waits on high to have compassion on*
*you.*
*For the LORD is a God of justice;*
*How blessed are all those who long for Him.*
—Isaiah 30:15–18

*One hand full of rest is better than two fists full of labor*
*and striving after wind.*
—Ecclesiastes 4:6

Find a quiet place where you can be alone for an hour.

In this assignment, you will rest with God. "Resting with God" doesn't mean, "Okay, I'm going to do nothing 'with God.'"

Read Luke 10:38–42. What was the difference between Martha and Mary? Martha was spinning like a top, "doing for God," while Mary "wasted her time" by listening to Jesus. To rest with Jesus involves:

1. Surrender: taking your hands off the wheel of control.

2. Receiving: His love and care for you, that all of your sins are forgiven, and there's no need to perform.

3. Allowing Him to minister to you: "He makes me lie down in green pastures; He leads me beside quiet

waters, He restores my soul." For many Christians, the 23rd Psalm is a quaint chapter with nice thoughts; they've never rested with God and allowed Him to restore them. They don't understand that the relationship is woven into the 23rd Psalm and that the Lord wants to minister to them.

4. Focusing your attention on Jesus and listening as Mary did.

5. Cessation of every attempt to work, strive, push, or earn God's love. Pleasing Him means resting with Him, with the intent of wanting to know Him and hear from Him.

Note that in Isaiah 30 we're told that "in quietness and trust is our strength." As you continue to do these exercises that involve connecting with God, His love will take a deeper root in your soul and provide strength, peace, and rest.

### A Night Away with Him

Find a Christian retreat center near you where you can stay overnight. There should be no TVs in the room or other distractions like an event or conference going on where a lot of people will be there. A place that is somewhat secluded so the only noise is the sound of nature is better.

Make plans to go away, alone, to the retreat center. Bring only your Bible, your journal, and your personal effects (some retreats don't have food so you might need to bring this as well).

Set your mind on making this time alone solely about seeking God; leave everything else behind, including problems at home, work, or family. If you have to, you can bring your phone for communication purposes, but stay away from laptops, iPads, or other electronic distractions, including social media.

After you settle in, ask the Lord to speak to you and show you what He wants you to do, wait for the answer, and roll with it. He may want you to wait, pray, worship, or He might bring a verse or passage from Scripture to your mind.

He may even just say "rest." On one of my solo visits to the retreat I frequent, I was worn out. It had been a hard week and I didn't have much left in the tank. To my surprise, I sensed God telling me to take a nap. Just Him showing me that He saw my need for rest ministered to me and deepened my love for Him once more.

I try to go alone for an overnight stay at a retreat once every six months. God speaks to me every time. It's always hard to go home, not because I don't want to be with my family, but because I've tasted heaven.

I spent eight years searching for freedom from sexual addiction. I tried everything man said to do, and in the end, I was still left with an empty heart. Once I became desperate and made the Lord my last hope, God started putting the message of seeking Him in front of me.

Once the light went on that I had been hungry for God all of my life and I went after Him with everything I had, He revealed Himself to me and flooded my heart with His love.

## DRAWING NEAR

My deepest desire is that you will know Him and experience His peace, rest, love, and care for you.

Of course, I would love to see your marriage restored too.

# NOTES

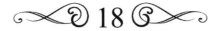

# 18

## God Shines through the Cracks

*I don't know any other wives who have gone through the pain of their husband's sexual sin. It's painful and awkward, and I feel very alone. I am praying that a woman could come alongside me for a while to help me with this new situation. I certainly don't want to develop any negative coping skills (depression, drinking, fighting with him, anger) as I walk this path. Could you please have someone get in touch with me for support?*

In 2000, when I first got into this ministry, surveys showed that 50 percent of Christian men were viewing pornography. Today, the numbers are at 66 percent.[2]

The porn epidemic in the church is growing. If two-thirds of Christian men are viewing porn, a huge swathe of wives need help coping and healing from their

---

[2] For more information on Christians and pornography use, please visit our website for updated statistics: www.roadtograce.net.

husband's sexual sin.

Most of these women feel utterly alone.

The comment I hear most from wives is, "I don't have anyone to talk to." Many keep their story a secret.

Years ago, I contacted a vendor for help with my first book. After I told her what the topic was, she broke down crying: she had lost her marriage to her husband's sex addiction. That scene has replayed multiple times over the years: I share my story or about the ministry, which encourages the other side to open up with theirs.

Often, they're the people you would have never guessed had an issue with sexual sin—the ones who look like they have it all together.

The church needs you to share your story. So do tens of thousands of other women with hurting hearts. The reason many women feel alone is because most of you are hiding your story instead of allowing God to minister through it. It's a self-perpetuating cycle that won't stop until Christian women come out of hiding, open up, and make themselves available to other women who are on the same path you've walked.

I don't want you to think I'm advocating that you dump your life's story on your family or on social media to the wrong audience. Nor am I saying that if you recently discovered your husband's sexual sin and are reeling and hurting that you should charge into ministry. None of this is wise.

However, if you're in a good place personally (regardless of where your marriage is), I encourage you to put your hand up as Isaiah did:

# GOD SHINES THROUGH THE CRACKS

*Then I heard the voice of the Lord, saying, "Whom shall
I send, and who will go for Us?" Then I said, "Here am
I. Send me!" He said, "Go, and tell this people . . ."*
—Isaiah 6:8–9

In God's word, you will find that effective ministry
often began when God sent His people, not when they
got fired up and decided to "do something good for God"
through the weakness of their flesh. Many Christians try
to charge the hill for God and make a mess because they
didn't go with Him, weren't ready, or were doing it for
their glory.

Some who God used powerfully resisted His call.
Moses told God to "go find someone else" (Exodus
4:13), while Jonah went the opposite direction and
suffered the consequences for his disobedience.

Some wives think they may be disqualified from
helping other women because their marriage isn't in the
best place, or they're divorced. Nothing could be further
from the truth. If you've been divorced because of your
husband's sexual sin, the church needs to hear your story
because you've paid the ultimate price. The body of
Christ needs to know the devastating consequences of
pornography and adultery to a marriage; it's not an issue
that should be ignored.

The Lord uses people who don't have it all together.
It just takes someone who is okay with being broken, a
dose of humility, and the willingness to show up and
allow God to minister through the cracks of their life.

We can get ministry backward. Many think that God
can't use them if they're broken or failed, but He blesses

others through them because of their sins and weaknesses.

My favorite disciple is Peter—the apostle who denied Christ. Peter gives me great hope because he failed miserably and Christ restored him.

I wouldn't write this book if I weren't willing to state publicly that I struggled with pornography and other sexual sin, committed adultery, and wounded my wife. If I were an "expert" with letters after my name who hadn't walked the path of recovery and healing, how much credibility would I have?

God shines through the cracks of our lives.

Covering them up is about us—trying to look good so others will be impressed. Allowing our cracks to be exposed gives God the glory and provides the opening for His light to shine through and minister to the broken.

If you're willing to say, "Here I am, Lord, I'm willing. Send me where you want to," in His time, He'll provide the opportunity.

Look for open doors to share your story, especially in one-on-one encounters. Pray for divine appointments. Consider approaching the women's ministry leader or the pastor of your church.

At Blazing Grace, we receive emails daily from hurting wives who need another woman to talk to. If you feel like the Lord might be leading you in that direction, please contact us so we can get you plugged in and helping others.

We need wives to lead our wives' phone groups, write blog posts, participate on the forums, and more.

Let's make it so that fewer women can say, "I don't

have anyone to talk to," shall we?

*Blessed be the God and Father of our Lord Jesus Christ,*
*the Father of mercies and God of all comfort, who*
*comforts us in all our affliction so that we will be able to*
*comfort those who are in any affliction with the comfort*
*with which we ourselves are comforted by God.*
—II Corinthians 1:3–4

# NOTES

# Bonus Material

## The Unwanted Chapter

I didn't want to write this chapter. Every marriage is precious, and I always want to offer hope and encourage you to persevere until your marriage is restored. I've seen God heal marriages that were on the verge of divorce. (One divorce was several days from being finalized in court when the Lord turned their hearts around.)

But the reality is there are some marriages that won't make it. The wife sets boundaries and consequences, gives her all, and supports her husband, yet he hardens his heart and throws himself deeper into sexual sin, and their relationship passes the point of no return. Some women are wounded so deeply they never recover (the wrong counsel didn't help) and the marriage is lost, even though the husband broke free.

If you're considering divorce, here are several points to think about:

If your husband is getting help, yet stumbling, there is still hope. As long as he's not having affairs or having sex outside of marriage with others, consider waiting a little longer to see how it plays out.

You might need to consider a divorce if:

Your husband ignores your boundaries and continually crashes through them, without regard to the consequences.

He's abusive verbally, or especially, physically, on an ongoing basis, and shows no signs of conviction or remorse. If he hits you, it would be best that you leave immediately and get the counsel of a professional with experience in spousal abuse.

You separated from him because he crossed your boundary of no sex with others outside of marriage, yet he continued to engage in sexual sin.

He refuses to get help.

He makes little to no effort to restore your relationship, other than occasionally saying something to placate you for the moment.

You continue to catch him in lies, or he makes promises he doesn't keep.

Your safe friend, who has been supportive of your efforts to heal your marriage, believes you've exhausted all of your options and divorce is all that's left.

You've gone to God and asked Him what to do, and believe He's saying it's time to close the door on the marriage.

Most or all of the indicators above are true.

If you're living with your husband, move out and spend time in prayer. If the Lord confirms you should let the marriage go, start looking for an attorney.

I hate it when a marriage fails because of sexual sin. As a child of divorce, I know that the damage and trauma divorce inflicts on a family is gut-wrenching. Many marriages would be healed if the church were willing to speak out boldly on sexual issues and provide clear answers.

It may be that divorce is the only way you can heal. If you're living with an abusive husband who continues to trample on your heart with his sexual sin and the way he treats you, there is no relationship. Staying might make it worse because you could put yourself and your kids in danger.

Once a man's heart goes dark, he can become evil and twisted, marked by rage, abuse, manipulation, and cruelty. You dare not stay with a man in that condition.

You were given the right to divorce your husband the first time he committed adultery, whether with porn or another person (Matthew 5:32).

You are not sinning by choosing to end an abusive relationship, in spite of what anyone says—including those in the church.

There are some in the church who might try to throw a guilt trip on you, even pastors, if you decide to end your marriage. They don't know the whole story or how hard you've tried, and have no right to be an armchair critic. Don't listen to them.

Not long ago, a wife in the South divorced her husband who was hooked on child porn, which is a felony in the US. What made me sick was when the leadership of her church rebuked her because she didn't follow their restoration procedure before filing. After the national news media caught wind of it, the leadership of her church backed down and apologized.

The Pharisees, those who care more about their rules and traditions than people, are alive and well in the church today. Don't listen to them. If you know God is calling you to a divorce, proceed.

Your healing process will include saying goodbye to your marriage and grieving what was lost. Continue to lean on the support of your trusted friend or group. Allow them to minister to you and support you.

If you don't have a support group, contact us so we can get you plugged in to our wives' groups.

Some husbands try to stop their wives from making the reason for the divorce public because they don't want their reputation blown. You need not feel guilty about exposing what happened; use wisdom and consider what is appropriate.

Some wives beat themselves up with what "they should or could have done." Their husband chose sexual sin and darkness; they neither encouraged it nor wanted it. Most wives do everything they can and more to make their marriage work.

*How much severer punishment do you think he will deserve who has trampled under foot the Son of God, and has regarded as unclean the blood of the covenant by which he was sanctified, and has insulted the Spirit of grace? —Hebrews 10:29*

## THE UNWANTED CHAPTER

*Do not be deceived, God is not mocked; for whatever a man sows, this he will also reap.*
—Galatians 6:7

The Lord doesn't compromise with those who chase sin. If your husband is abusive to you and persists in sexual sin, it's impossible for his relationship with the Lord to be in the right place, no matter what position in the church he holds. He's in a dangerous position spiritually, with serious eternal ramifications if he continues on his path.

You may have made some mistakes along the way. I don't know of anyone who gets everything right when it comes to something as hard and painful as recovering from adultery. Nevertheless, if your husband is the man I've described in this chapter, you can stand before God with a clear conscience.

# NOTES

# Lies and Truth

This is the material mentioned in Chapter 14 with the lies you might have bought in to about yourself or God, contrasted with the truth from God's word.

**Your parents or others may have:**

- **Been disappointed in you, but...**

  God isn't disappointed in you, His child, no matter what you've done. *In fact, He's waiting to throw a party for you.*

Read the story of the Prodigal Son in Luke 15:11–32. The son deeply insulted his father by asking for his inheritance up front, which was the same as saying he wished his father was dead.

The son then blew all of his inheritance on prostitutes and partying. In spite of this, when his son returned home, his father threw a party for him! Although the son had messed up badly, his father loved him deeply; not one word of disappointment or judgment was spoken.

No matter where you are today, God is waiting for you to come to Him so He can shower you with an extravagant party of grace.

- **Been distant, but...**

God has always been close to you.

*"But as for me, the nearness of God is my good; I have made the Lord GOD my refuge."*
—Psalm 73:28

You may have been neglected growing up. Perhaps one of your parents died and you've always wondered, "Where were you, God?"

You struggle with the idea that God is around, or that you matter enough for Him to be around for you. He has always been near, and He's close to you now. Ask Him to reveal His presence to you.

- **Been unapproachable, but...**

God wants you to come to Him.

*"Therefore let us draw near with confidence to the throne of grace, so that we may receive mercy and find grace to help in time of need."*
—Hebrews 4:16

God wants you to come to Him because He loves you and wants to help you.

He's not like broken men and women, who get irritated, impatient, and short-tempered if we don't have it all together or mess up.

Mercy and comfort await you at the throne of grace; you need not be afraid to approach Him.

- **Been absent, but…**

The Lord will never leave you.

> *"For He Himself has said, I WILL NEVER DESERT YOU, NOR WILL I EVER FORSAKE YOU.'"*
> —Hebrews 13:5

> *"'Am I a God Who is near,' declares the Lord, 'and not a God far off? . . . Do I not fill the heaven and the earth?'"*
> —Jeremiah 23:23–24

God is not a workaholic father or mother who is never around. You matter to Him, and He is here for you now.

- **Rejected you, but…**

God has completely accepted you because of the cross of Christ.

> *"Therefore there is now no condemnation for those who are in Christ Jesus."* —Romans 8:1

*"Therefore, accept one another, just as Christ*
*also accepted us to the glory of God."*
—Romans 15:7

The cross is the most powerful event in history. At the cross, Jesus wiped the slate clean and provided abundant entry into heaven for those of us who believe in Him. His acceptance of you is not based on anything but His sacrificial death, and your sin can't erase His acceptance of you. He will not reject you if you approach Him.

- **Abandoned you, but...**

God has taken you up.

*"For my father and my mother have forsaken me,*
*but the LORD will take me up."* —Psalm 27:10

*"A father of the fatherless and a judge for the*
*widows, is God in His holy habitation."* —Psalm
68:5

*"For He Himself has said, 'I WILL NEVER*
*DESERT YOU, NOR WILL I EVER FORSAKE*
*YOU.'"* —Hebrews 13:5

Maybe your parents divorced, and you assumed that "Mom or Dad didn't stick around because of me."

Perhaps you were adopted, and suffer with the idea that you were cast aside, unwanted, and rejected.

Or maybe you were abandoned to the streets at an early age. God will never abandon you, and I believe He's drawing you to Him right now.

- **Been a perfectionist, demanding the same from you for their approval or love, but...**

    God knows you're a mess (Romans 3:23) and can never be perfect, and has showered you with the free gift of His grace.

    *"For by grace you have been saved through faith; and that not of yourselves, it is the gift of God."*
    —Ephesians 2:8

    *"And hope does not disappoint, because the love of God has been poured out within our hearts through the Holy Spirit who was given to us."*
    —Romans 5:5

God knows you've sinned and will never be perfect. He doesn't point fingers, reject, bash you with Bible verses, or demand perfection, like other broken, imperfect men and women have done.

You can stop trying to measure up to an impossible standard and accept the big, brightly wrapped gift of grace God has for you.

- **Abused you, but...**

God wants to comfort you, if you let Him.

> *"I, even I, am He who comforts you."*
> —Isaiah 51:12

He comforts the traumatized, the abused, and the neglected. You won't get hurt if you approach Him; He's not out to use you. He will comfort you, if you will take a chance and drop your guard.

- **Failed to love you in word or deed, but...**

God loves you passionately:

> *"But God, who is rich in mercy, because of His great love with which He loved us, even when we were dead in trespasses made us alive together with Christ."*
> —Ephesians 2:4, NKJV

> *"Just as the Father has loved Me, I have also loved you; abide in My love."*
> —John 15:9

*"This is My commandment, that you love one another, just as I have loved you."*
—John 15:12

*"But I would feed you with the finest of the wheat and with honey from the rock I would satisfy you."*
—Psalm 81:16

*"For God so loved the world, that He gave His only begotten Son, that whoever believes in Him shall not perish, but have eternal life."*
—John 3:16

*"Because Your lovingkindness is better than life."*
—Psalm 63:3

# NOTES

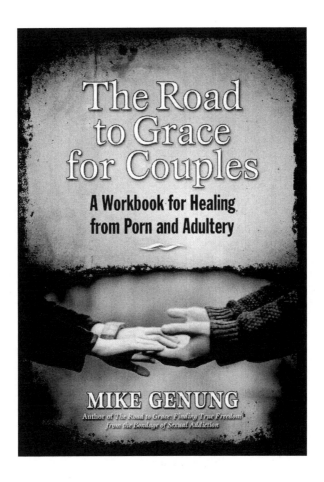

The following is a chapter from Mike Genung's book, *The Road to Grace for Couples: A Workbook for Healing from Porn and Adultery.*

This is a workbook husbands and wives can work through together to restore their marriage. Assignments are provided with each chapter.

To order, go to www.roadtograce.net.

# Finding Your Best Friend

This should be the easiest, and hopefully, one of the more enjoyable chapters of this book. When a marriage blows up from sexual sin, all sense of friendship, fun, and adventure in the relationship can be lost. Today's assignment: date your spouse once a week for the next three months.

"Once a week for the next three months?! We have jobs, kids, families, and bills to pay. How 'bout once a month? We've been married for years and don't need it; it's not like when we were dating before we got married."

Yes, you need it.

Think back to when you first met your spouse. How crazy and over the top did you go for him or her? Remember chapter six of this workbook. What's the biggest priority in your life, second only to God? When's the last time you went overboard for your spouse? How do you think they would feel if you did? Loved? Cared for? Like they're a big priority to you?

A while back, Michelle and I were having a rough patch in our marriage. We'd drifted so far apart that neither of us knew how to get our relationship going again. It was so bad that Michelle wondered aloud whether our marriage had run its course. Our relationship was fading, and we desperately needed to make changes.

We started going out once a week. Money was tight, so we often met at our church café where meals were inexpensive. Occasionally, we went to a theater where movies that have been out for a while were one dollar for a ticket. Or we just walked around a mall and had fun window-shopping.

The effect on our relationship was amazing. We started laughing again and having fun for the first time in years. The friendship we'd lost resurfaced; wounds started to heal. Life got better.

This came about from making a conscientious decision that no matter what it took, we were going to make our marriage a priority and rebuild it. We both worked, had four kids, and little money, but we didn't let that stop us.

When my relationship with my wife is on the rocks, life sucks. Work's a chore, I want to hang my head at home, and feel like a poser in church. I don't sleep well. God made Michelle and me as one flesh—we're not supposed to feel like everything's okay when our marriage is hurting.

Perhaps there is still resistance.

"My kids/family/friends/church/office need me. I don't have time." Yeah, and so does your spouse; they come first. If your marriage is dying and your church is guilt-tripping you about not "doing enough for God," tell them no, or find another church. Yes, your kids need you, but don't you think your kids want to see Mom and Dad having fun together instead of fighting—or worse? How about the office? I know we're living in tough economic times, but at some point, you'll either need to make the time to date your spouse, or tell your employer you can't do sixty-hour workweeks.

If you have kids, get a babysitter. If you can't afford one, the teens in your church may be willing to do it as ministry. Ask around to see what's available.

If money's tight, get creative. You don't need an expensive restaurant every week, just a place where you can get away from everyone and focus on getting to know each other.

When you go out, turn your cell phones off. Give each other your best; no distractions allowed.

If your kids are in school, meeting for lunch during the workweek is an easy way to avoid the need for a babysitter.

I strongly encourage you to plan a weekend away for the two of you. It will cost a little more, but every investment made in your marriage will provide an excellent return on your money and time.

When you're on a date, refrain from discussing kids, work, and family. Focus on each other. Share your dreams. Talk from the heart, but if possible, try to set recovery topics aside. Have fun. Sometimes we can get so deeply immersed in support groups, counseling, and all that heavy stuff that we forget what it feels like just to unwind and have fun. Your marriage needs this.

Today's action step is to set a dating plan. Work together to find the best way to make it happen, and start this week.

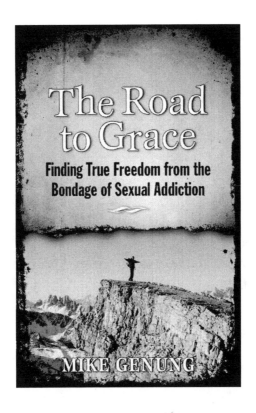

*I've read most of the highest rated books on sexual addiction, and this is by far the best. Mike addresses the core issues we need to work through; this is a must-read for anyone who struggles with sexual sin and accepting God's love and grace. Well done.*

—Brandon

*I have just finished reading The Road to Grace, and it is everything and more than I expected! I plan on rereading it starting tomorrow. Thank you. The book is changing my life.*

—Joe

*Your book was amazing. I've read several sex addiction books, and yours is the best. Your suffering and God's grace made this book powerful. It covers every aspect of sexual addiction from the steps to recovery to mending the marriage.*

—Shelley Lubben

*Your book has done a great work of healing in my husband's life. We read it together. Each chapter, he faces more of his past and heals those wounds. God bless you for your willingness to expose your life to everyone.*

—K.B.

**Features:**

- Biblical methods for overcoming sexual temptation.
- Healing from shame.
- How to stop a masturbation habit.
- Dealing with the core issues that drive sexual sin.
- Understanding and receiving the love of God in the heart.
- Healing for wives.
- How to restore a marriage that's been scarred by sexual sin.
- Excellent for use in support groups.

Available at www.roadtgrace.net.

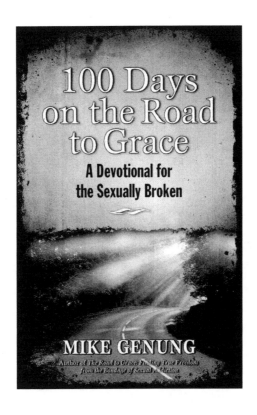

*One of our translators was really blessed by your book. It enabled her to look into her past and receive healing . . . she wanted you to know that it was a blessing for her.*

—Phil P., Austria, director of a ministry that translated *100 Days* into German.

*Your books enabled me to start turning the corner on a long road of darkness that enslaved me for 50 years.*

—J.M.

*100 Days on the Road to Grace: A Devotional for the Sexually Broken* offers a collection of 100 powerful readings that expand on Mike Genung's first book.

**Topics include:**

- The path to freedom from porn and sexual addiction.
- Keys to rebuilding your character.
- Coping with emotions such as anger, depression, and fear.
- Rebuilding trust and bringing healing to your marriage and family.
- Bitterness and forgiveness.
- Breaking the bondage of self.
- Spiritual warfare.
- Revitalizing the relationship with God.
- Living a life that counts for eternity.
- And many more.

If you're hungry for God and want more than just freedom from sexual sin, this book is for you. Available at www.roadtograce.net

Mike Genung can be reached at:
Blazing Grace
PO Box 25763
Colorado Springs, CO 80936

www.blazinggrace.org
email@blazinggrace.org

Your comments and questions are welcome.


See www.roadtograce.net and blazinggrace.org
for information on Mike Genung's books,
articles, mp3s of the Blazing Grace Radio show,
information on future books, and more.

# Acknowledgments

My wife, Michelle, for working through the pain of my adultery with me and rebuilding our marriage.

Robin Williams, who leads our wives' support groups, for encouraging me to write this book.

Rita and Barb, for their suggestions.

Every hurting wife who has contacted us at Blazing Grace looking for help. Your stories are the reason for this book.

The ladies who serve the women in our wives' support groups. God has used all of you to mend hurting hearts and restore marriages.